BEADING WITH WORLD BEADS

BEADING WITH WORLD BEADS

Beautiful Jewelry, Simple Techniques

Ray Hemachandra

LARK BOOKS

A Division of Sterling Publishing Co., Inc.
New York / London

Senior Editor
Ray Hemachandra

Editor
Larry Shea

Assistant Editor
Mark Bloom

Developmental Assistance
Beth Sweet

Art Director
Megan Kirby

Art Production
Carol Morse

Illustrator
J'aime Allene Perkins

Photographer
Stewart O'Shields

Cover Designer
Chris Bryant

Library of Congress Cataloging-in-Publication Data

Beading with world beads : beautiful jewelry, simple techniques /
Ray Hemachandra.
      p. cm.
  Includes index.
   ISBN 978-1-60059-298-0 (hc-plc with jacket : alk. paper)
  1. Beadwork. 2. Jewelry making. I. Hemachandra, Ray.
   TT860.B333855 2009
   739.27--dc22
                                        2008036241

10 9 8 7 6 5 4 3 2 1

First Edition

Published by Lark Books, A Division of
Sterling Publishing Co., Inc.
387 Park Avenue South, New York, NY 10016

© 2009, Lark Books

Distributed in Canada by Sterling Publishing,
c/o Canadian Manda Group, 165 Dufferin Street
Toronto, Ontario, Canada M6K 3H6

Distributed in the United Kingdom by GMC Distribution Services,
Castle Place, 166 High Street, Lewes, East Sussex, England BN7 1XU

Distributed in Australia by Capricorn Link (Australia) Pty Ltd.,
P.O. Box 704, Windsor, NSW 2756 Australia

If you have questions or comments about this book, please contact:
Lark Books
67 Broadway
Asheville, NC 28801
828-253-0467

Manufactured in China

ISBN 13: 978-1-60059-298-0

For information about custom editions, special sales, premium and corporate
purchases, please contact Sterling Special Sales Department at 800-805-5489
or specialsales@sterlingpub.com.

contents

introduction

Many of the borders and divisions that have historically separated the world's peoples have melted away. Trade, travel, and the Internet make even the other side of the world not that distant anymore. As international trends affect everything from cuisine to clothing design to popular culture, I see the same wonderful and inspiring dynamic in craft sensibilities. Today's crafters are exposed to the influences and craft traditions of cultures from around the globe. World Internet communities of crafters abound in every niche, and simple image finds on search engines can produce a rich crop of craft ideas. The result is a multicultural bonanza—a melting pot of craft practices that yields innovative combinations of materials and influences.

Beaders are especially open to world and ethnic inspirations. These crafters have long sought beads from other cultures, and the availability of such beads—both authentic beads from many areas of the world and outstanding replicas primarily from China and India—offers unprecedented bounty to them. Beads are part of the origins of every culture, and bead stores are exotic places of exploration and discovery. When I visit a good bead store these days, it feels a lot like a trip to the United Nations gift shop when I was growing up in New York in the 1970s. Signs indicating countries of origin or influence are paired with most of the beads. Like a child looking at fantastic new toys and tchotchkes never seen before, beaders experience constant delight and marvelous surprise as they pore over each store's array of beads.

What it means for beaders is the opportunity to discover and create infinite new possibilities and combinations of beads and designs. We mean to bring you both ideas and inspiration with this book. First, you'll read about world-bead traditions, get tips on selecting world beads, and learn about beadwork tools and techniques. Then, look through the heart of the book to find the jewelry projects that captivate you. Fifteen talented beaders have created more than 35 jewelry designs that celebrate the rich diversity of the modern multicultural world.

Many of the jewelry pieces have an overall ethnic or world flavor, and some simply incorporate beads from a bounty of global destinations. The splendid Year of the Dragon features a central Chinese brass zodiac talisman on a necklace popping with cinnabar beads and Swarovski crystal pearls (page 51). Golden Dunes Bracelet evokes the South Pacific with a rich jangle of conch shell beads and mother-of-pearl nuggets (page 48). Four thousand African heishi trade beads are strung to form an astonishingly sleek, modern necklace called Touch of the Ivory Coast (page 22). And Temple Gate Bracelet mixes beads made of Thai silver, Czech glass, and Chinese porcelain to create a piece of jewelry with a regal look and an international soul (page 61).

All the designs are meant to spark your creativity. Once you've made a few of the projects, consider becoming a bead-store globetrotter in search of your next beading adventure. You'll be inspired by the world beads—and traditions—you discover and make your own.

a tour around the beading world

Before beads were used as gorgeous adornments, accessories, and collectibles, they served our prehistoric ancestors' desire for protection from unexplainable forces of nature. These early beads were made from stone, teeth, bone, wood, and seeds. Archaeologists have excavated beads thought to be almost 40,000 years old.

As trade routes developed and spanned the globe, the exchange of beads between cultures flourished. Clay beads from the shores of Greece were bartered for silver beads in the markets of Egypt, and glass beads from Italy were exchanged for ivory and gold in Africa. Huge ships sailed the seas, laden with stores of beads and bound for distant shores. Beads were the tradesman's currency.

Beads have long been powerful elements of religious faith as well. The word bead originates from the Middle English term *bede*, meaning "prayer." Rosaries, prayer beads, and prayer scrolls for worshipers of many faiths were often at the forefront of jewelry design.

A myriad of different bead traditions has evolved in different parts of the world. The traditional jewelry of Africa is vibrant and diverse, reflecting the continent's many peoples and customs. North Africa is known for its silverwork. Egyptian beads are famous for their use of lapis lazuli, gold, turquoise, and semiprecious stones; today, Egypt also is a source of clay beads, as well as delicate silver and gold filigree.

The batik bone beads of East Africa, most often created in Kenya, can be identified by their large round shapes and contrasting geometric designs. West African countries, particularly Ghana, are known for their recycled glass beads. Unlike the flameworked glass beads of Europe, Ghanaian tribes collect glass from various sources, crush it into a fine powder, and fire it in a mold.

Clay and sand-cast beads from West Africa

Cow Bone Necklace **with batik beads, page 42**

Venetian trade beads

Seven-layer chevron beads made in 18th-century Venice

Tibetan turquoise and crushed coral beads from Nepal

A silver hand-stamped bead, made by a Jewish silversmith in Yemen

During the Italian Renaissance, Venice established itself as the undisputed center of glassmaking. Italian glass artists practiced their craft on the island of Murano and fiercely guarded the secrets of their techniques. Although these methods are no longer quite so mysterious today, Murano glass is still crafted in Venice, and the traditions of chevron, millefiori, blown glass, and gold foil glass beads have been handed down through generations of Venetian artists.

The faceted and foiled glass beads of the Czech Republic have also long been held in high regard. In addition to innovative flower beads, many classic styles and designs of Czech beads remain in great demand today. Similarly, the traditional silver work of the Middle East continues to flourish, along with the production of amulets and pendants.

In India and nearby countries such as Tibet and Nepal, jewelry is an essential part of everyday adornment. Colorful glass beads and intricate silverwork are distributed from the Indian subcontinent, and natural beads made of bone, wood, and nuts are often decorated with traditional Indian designs. In Tibet, turquoise is thought to protect wearers from evil and is often accompanied by amber and coral in religious jewelry.

China is widely regarded as the leading producer of beads made from semiprecious gemstones, and hand painted porcelain and cloisonné are standing tributes to the country's exquisitely detailed beadwork. Balinese silver techniques include engraving, filigree, hammering, embossing, and granulation, which can often be found in large round beads and pendants. The bead industry in the Philippines is young, having only begun in the mid-1900s, but the country's wood, shell, stone, and painted beads already are avidly collected.

Bali-style silver beads from India

In Central and South America, gold is king. Throughout history, people worshiped the Sun God, known by many names and faces, by wearing flat golden disks to reflect the sun's rays. Jadeite, turquoise, heishi, mother of pearl, and other natural beads are also significant in this region. In Peru, ceramic beads are hand-painted in exquisite traditional Peruvian designs.

Chinese cloisonné and ceramic beads

Assorted Czech beads

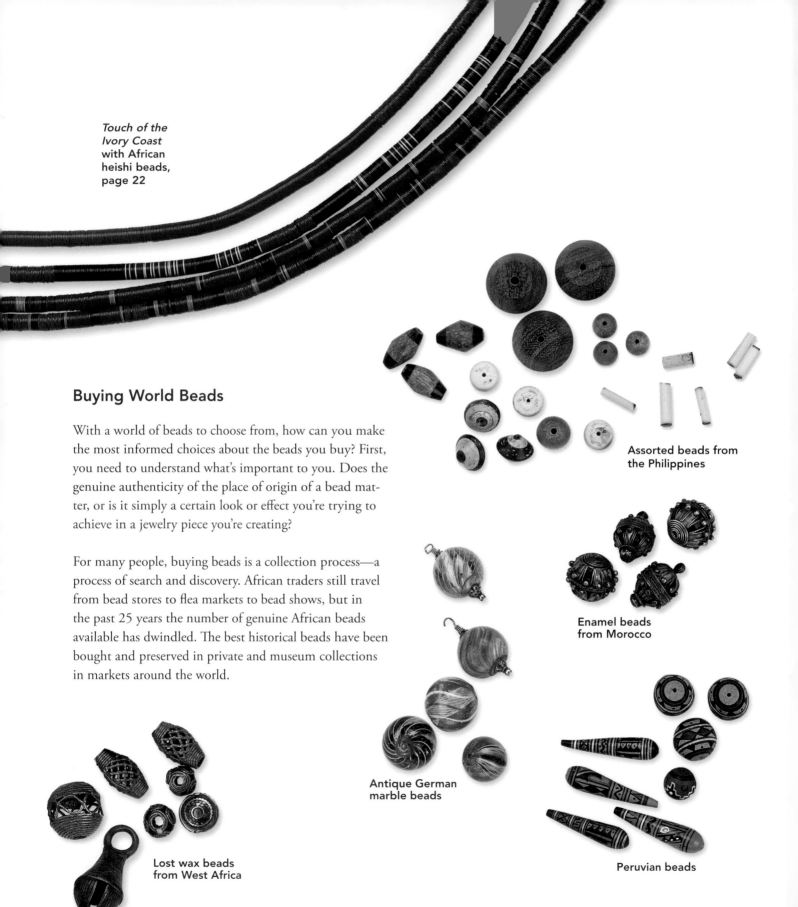

Touch of the Ivory Coast **with African heishi beads, page 22**

Buying World Beads

With a world of beads to choose from, how can you make the most informed choices about the beads you buy? First, you need to understand what's important to you. Does the genuine authenticity of the place of origin of a bead matter, or is it simply a certain look or effect you're trying to achieve in a jewelry piece you're creating?

For many people, buying beads is a collection process—a process of search and discovery. African traders still travel from bead stores to flea markets to bead shows, but in the past 25 years the number of genuine African beads available has dwindled. The best historical beads have been bought and preserved in private and museum collections in markets around the world.

Assorted beads from the Philippines

Enamel beads from Morocco

Antique German marble beads

Lost wax beads from West Africa

Peruvian beads

Venetian-style blown glass beads from China

Because genuine trade beads—the older beads that were essentially used as currency—are scarce today, those authentic beads still available on the market are increasingly expensive. But less-expensive reproductions are so well made that even experienced beaders and store owners struggle to tell the difference between the replicas and the real things.

In fact, the vast majority of beads available today are made in India or China. So, the question is very personal: Does the difference between the genuine article and a first-rate imitation matter to you? Would you rather pay more for a Balinese-style metal bead made in Bali or pay less for a very good replica—a Balinese-style plastic bead made in China? Does a bead's history matter to you, especially if you're making a rosary for prayers or using quality gemstone beads because of their metaphysical or superstitious meanings? If authenticity matters, your best bet is to buy from a reputable retailer or dealer with extensive experience and training. Look for one who works hard to be certain about the provenance—where and when a bead was made—of every item offered.

Even if you learn a bead isn't authentic, do you still love it? Will it contribute to your design intent with a specific piece of jewelry? The best situation is when you've been told all the facts; then, if you're happy with the bead, buy it. The meaning it will carry is the meaning you assign to it.

Assorted beads from India

Chinese cinnabar beads

Bali-style metal beads from India

Chinese-style beads from India

materials and tools

The next stop on your journey to making stunning jewelry with world beads is gathering the tools and materials you'll need. In order to create the best showcase for your beads, invest in the best materials and tools you can. You'll be able to find just about any item mentioned below at your local high-quality bead shop or large craft store, and you can also track down these materials online and at most retail bead shows. World beads are just that—beads from around the world—so keep your eyes peeled for unique bead finds on your travels.

The Beads

When it comes to world beads, the possibilities range just about as far and wide as the globe they come from. The following is a bit of information on some of the types of beads you'll encounter. These categories apply to both ethnic and non-ethnic beads. You can decide to use only ethnic beads, or join together whatever types of beads strike your fancy to make beautiful world-bead jewelry projects.

When it comes to world beads and their ancient traditions, we often think first of beads with a more direct connection to the natural world than the manufactured products that fill our lives. These beads are sometimes worked by hand in fine detail and sometimes left in a nearly natural state. Such varieties include *bone beads* and *horn beads*. Beads that derive from the earth's bounty include *wooden beads* and *nut and seed beads*. And *clay beads*, among the earliest types made, literally come from the earth itself.

Tagua nut beads from the Amazon rainforest

Rudraksha seed beads

Bone and horn beads from India

Olive wood beads from Greece

Other beads are made from natural materials long treasured for their beauty and rarity. *Semiprecious gemstone beads* come in every size, shape, and color you can imagine. Most stone beads are hewn by hand, and their prices range from inexpensive on up, depending on the availability, grade, and cut of the stone.

Freshwater pearl beads are created naturally by freshwater mollusks. You can find them in a surprising variety of colors and shapes, because each kind of species produces a different sort of pearl. The characteristic uneven surface differentiates a freshwater pearl from an ocean pearl.

An assortment of pearl beads

As people developed processes for working with metal and glass, many more stunning bead varieties appeared. *Metal beads* can be machine-stamped, made with molds, or handmade. Depending on your needs and budget, you can find them in precious and base-metal varieties, including sterling silver, gold-filled, silver- and gold-plated (over brass), vermeil (gold over sterling silver), brass, and pewter.

Chinese coin beads　　　　**Bali-style beads**

Lapis lazuli beads from Afghanistan

Czech glass beads

Seed and bugle beads

Pressed-glass beads are made by pouring molten glass into molds and pressing the molds into shapes. Because the finest pressed-glass beads often come from the Czech Republic, these beads are sometimes called "Czech glass." Typical shapes of pressed-glass beads include leaves and flowers.

Lampworked beads are created by heating the end of a glass rod over a very hot flame until it melts, and then capturing the molten glass onto a thin spinning wire (a mandrel). You can find commercially made beads of this type; for a stunning focal bead, look for a one-of-a-kind lampworked bead from one of the many artists working in this field today.

Crystal beads are made from leaded glass and are cut in a way designed for producing maximum brilliance. The finest crystal beads come from Austria.

Above, we mentioned beads made from natural seeds. The *seed beads* you'll find in bead and craft stores are actually small glass beads made by cutting long, thin tubes of glass into tiny pieces. The most common sizes are between 6/0 and 14/0 (largest to smallest) and they come in a vast array of colors. Manufactured seed beads are primarily made in the Czech Republic and Japan and come in three popular types: Czech seed beads are somewhat flat like a donut; Japanese seed beads have a taller profile and are fairly uniform from bead to bead; and cylinder beads have thinner walls than other seed beads and are very uniform in shape. *Bugle beads* are longer, cylindrical glass beads that are also manufactured in the Czech Republic and Japan.

Crystal beads

Leather cord

Silk Road,
page 78

Stringing Materials

Finding the right material to string your beads on is essential for creating a long-lasting, good-looking piece of jewelry. Different materials can also create a different look or feel to match the types of beads you've chosen.

Beading line, also known as braided thread, is a braided nylon thread that's extremely strong and durable and can be knotted. It's an especially good choice for working with crystal beads because it doesn't abrade easily. It's generally available in clear, white, moss, and dark gray and comes in 6- to 20-pound test weights.

Beading thread is a very pliable thread made of nylon. It's fairly strong and you can find it in a wide variety of colors. Some beading threads come pre-waxed, but if yours doesn't, coat it liberally with wax or thread conditioner.

Chains are made up of connected loops of wire. The loops can come in several forms, including round, oval, twisted, and hammered.

Flexible beading wire is primarily used for stringing beads. It's produced by twisting dozens of strands of tiny stainless steel wires together and then applying a nylon coating. Secure this type of wire with crimp beads.

Leather cord is a good choice for a simple, natural look. It comes in many colors and widths. Much of the cord on the market today isn't really even leather but a type of synthetic. Use scissors to cut the end of leather cord at an angle, and you'll find it's easier to string beads onto it.

Metal wire comes in a range of widths, but 18- to 26-gauge (the smaller the number, the thicker the wire) are the sizes used most often for beading. Metal wire comes in a number of materials and varieties; the most common ones used to make fine jewelry are sterling silver and gold-filled.

Beading thread

Beading wire

Findings

These pieces, usually made of metal, help keep your jewelry together and secure.

Clasps connect wire ends to keep a necklace or bracelet in place. Among the most common types:

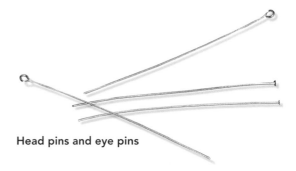

Head pins and eye pins

• *Box clasps* have one half that's comprised of a hollow box. The other half is a tab that clicks into the box to lock the clasp.
• *Hook-and-eye clasps* have one half that's shaped like a hook, and the other half like a loop, or "eye." The hook passes through the eye to secure the clasp.

Clasps

• *Fish-hook clasps* are shaped like a J and are usually used in a design that has a chain at the other end. The clasp hooks into a link of the chain to secure the piece.
• *Spring-ring clasps* are made up of a circle with a small spring-loaded lever that opens and shuts the circle. They are usually small and used only for lightweight pieces.
• *Toggle clasps* have one half that looks like a ring; the other half is shaped like a bar and is passed through the ring to secure the clasp.

Cones are used at the end of a piece of multi-strand jewelry in order to hide knots. Usually made of metal, they come in a variety of sizes and styles.

Cones

Crimp tubes and *crimp beads* are used to connect beading wire to a finding. *Crimp covers* are beads you open up and then close over the crimp beads to hide them.

Earring findings are the metal pieces that attach an earring design to your earlobe. They include a jump-ring-like loop onto which you can add an earring dangle. They come in different shapes, including French ear wires, which look like upside-down U shapes, and lever backs, which are similar to French ear wires but have a safety catch on the back to hold the earring in place.

Earring findings

Eye pins are used to make beaded links. They are made with straight pieces of wire with a simple loop at one end.

Head pins are used for stringing beads to make dangles. Simple head pins are straight wires with a tiny disk at one end to hold beads in place, while ball-end head pins have a sphere at one end.

Jump rings are circular loops of wire used to connect parts of a piece of jewelry. They come in open and soldered-closed versions. *Split rings* are a more secure form of jump ring. They are formed like tiny key rings.

Jump rings

Other Materials

Here are a few other materials you may need to complete great world-bead projects.

Beeswax and *thread conditioner* are used to prepare thread before stitching. They can help ease thread tension and ensure the thread doesn't fray.

Glue is sometimes used to attach metal to metal or to secure knots. Jeweler's clear adhesive cement and two-part epoxy are the most popular kinds of glue among beaders.

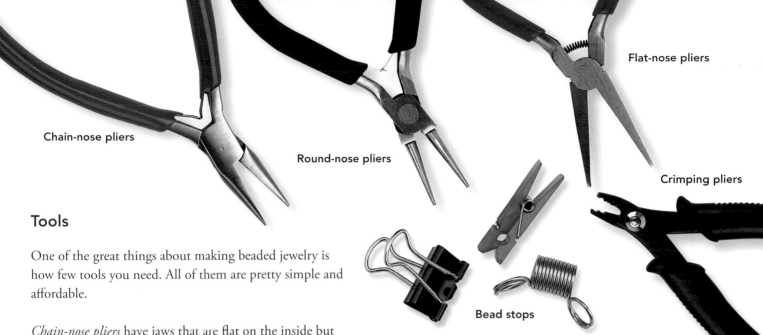

Chain-nose pliers

Round-nose pliers

Flat-nose pliers

Crimping pliers

Bead stops

Tools

One of the great things about making beaded jewelry is how few tools you need. All of them are pretty simple and affordable.

Chain-nose pliers have jaws that are flat on the inside but taper to a point on the outside. This type also comes in a bent version that's handy for grasping hard-to-reach places. *Flat-nose pliers* have jaws that are flat on the inside and feature a square nose. *Round-nose pliers* have cylindrical jaws that taper to a very fine point.

Crimping pliers are used to attach crimp beads and crimp tubes to beading wire.

Jeweler's wire cutters have very sharp blades that come to a point. One side of the pliers leaves a V-shaped cut, the other side leaves a flat (or flush) cut.

To sand wire smooth, *emery boards* can be used. *Metal hand files* or *needle files* can be used for smoothing wire ends.

You will often need *tape measures* or *rulers* to determine where to cut wire and thread. They're also helpful for checking jewelry lengths and bead and finding sizes. Find ones that have both standard and metric markings.

Safety glasses protect your eyes from flying pieces when cutting wire.

Other Beading Tools

Besides the basic jewelry tools above, a few other tools are helpful when beading.

Bead stops or *strong clips* are used to keep your beads from sliding off the end of the stringing material while you bead. They're most often used with flexible beading wire.

Beading mats are used to make sure your beads don't roll off your work surface and onto the floor. *Beading boards* are manufactured boards used to align beads in place as you work, particularly when making pieces with multiple strands.

Beading needles are extremely thin pieces of stiff wire that have a tiny hole on one end and a very sharp point on the other. The most popular types are English beading needles, which are especially thin and long, and sharp needles, which have a stronger body and are somewhat shorter.

Embroidery scissors are very sharp scissors with pointed blades and are used for cutting beading thread.

Thread burners, or *lighters*, help hide the clipped ends of synthetic threads by melting them into a tiny ball. They have a wire end that, once warmed up, can be placed against the end of the thread so that the thread melts away. You can also use a lighter for this job, but it won't be as precise.

basic techniques

Even if you're new to beading, you'll discover that it's really easy to make beautiful beaded jewelry right from the start. There are many different beading techniques, but you only need to know the following to complete the world-bead projects in this book.

Wireworking

Bending and shaping wire is a simple way to keep parts of your bead projects connected, add a design flourish—or both.

A few words on working with wire: *flush cutting* wire involves using the flat, or flush, side of the wire cutters to make the cut so the wire end is flat. *Filing* and *sanding* are done as needed to smooth rough wire ends. Use a flat metal file or emery paper for this, touching the wire occasionally as you go to check for any rough spots.

Coiling, or tightly wrapping, wire is used for attaching one wire to another, creating decorative coils, and making jump rings. To do this, grasp the base (a thick wire, dowel, or knitting needle) tightly in one hand. Hold the wrapping wire with your other hand and make one wrap. Reposition your hands so you can continue to wrap the wire around the base wire, making tight revolutions.

Wire spirals are used primarily for decoration, but they can also keep beads from sliding off the end of wire. Use your round-nose pliers to make a small loop at the end of the wire. Use chain- or flat-nose pliers to grasp the loop flat within the jaws so the edge of the loop sticks out slightly. Use your fingers to push the straight wire so it curves around the loop (photo 1). Adjust the wire's position within the pliers so you can curve more wire around the spiral. Repeat until you reach the desired width (photo 2).

photo 1

photo 2

Wire loops are used often in beading projects and can be either *simple* or *wrapped*.

Start a *simple loop* by using chain-nose pliers to make a 90° bend ⅜ inch (9 mm) from the end of the wire; or, if you're using the loop to secure a bead (as with a bead dangle), make a 90° bend right at the top of the bead and cut the wire to ⅜ inch (9 mm), as in photo 3.

Use round-nose pliers to grasp the wire end and roll the pliers until the wire touches the 90° bend (photo 4).

photo 3

photo 4

Bone and Sinew Earrings,
page 26

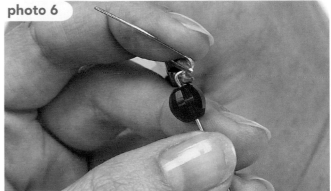

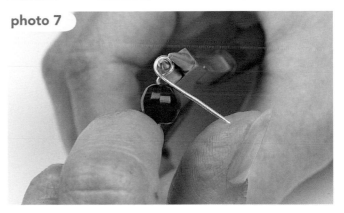

You begin a *wrapped loop* by using chain-nose pliers to make a 90° bend in the wire 2 inches (3.9 mm) from one wire end (or ¼ inch [6 mm] from the top of a bead) (photo 5).

Use round nose pliers to grasp the bend and shape the wire over the pliers' top jaw (photo 6).

Reposition the pliers so the bottom jaw is in the loop and swing the wire underneath to form a loop (photo 7).

Use chain-nose pliers or your fingers to wrap the wire in a tight coil down the stem (photo 8). Trim the excess wire close to the wrap, and use chain-nose pliers to tighten the wire end.

Once you've made a wrapped loop, it's easy to attach it to another loop or chain link. First form the loop, pass the wire end through the place you want to attach it, and then make the wrap. The loops will be permanently attached.

Working with Jump Rings

Be sure to always open or close a jump ring with two pairs of pliers, one positioned on each side of the split. Push one pair of pliers away from you, and pull the other one toward you to open a ring (photo 9). The ring opens laterally, instead of horizontally, which can weaken the wire. You can also use this method to open any kind of wire loop.

Stringing Beads

Now we get to the really easy part: stringing on the beads. Just pass the thread or wire through a bead, and you've got it!

Crimping wire is a stringing technique you use to attach wire to a finding (like a clasp). You start by stringing one crimp bead and the finding. Pass the wire back through the crimp bead in the opposite direction. Next, slide the crimp bead against the finding so it's snug, but not so tight that the wire can't move freely. Squeeze the crimp bead with the back U-shaped notch in a pair of crimping pliers (photo 10).

Turn the crimp bead at a 90° angle, and nestle it into the front notch. Gently squeeze the bead so it collapses on itself into a nicely-shaped tube (photo 11).

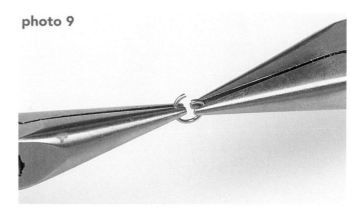
photo 9

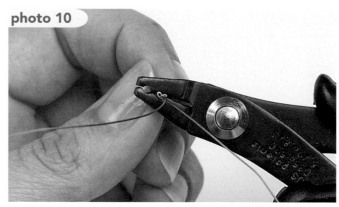
photo 10

photo 11

Eastern Memories,
page 116

Knotting

You will need to make some simple knots in these projects, and being able to make knots is a handy skill to have.

Overhand knots are formed by making a loop with the thread, passing the thread end through the loop, and pulling tight (figure 1).

Square knots are formed by first making an overhand knot, right end over left end, and finishing with another overhand knot, this time left end over right end (figure 2).

Surgeon's knots are extremely secure square knots. They are basically made the same way as a square knot, but when you make your first overhand knot, wrap the thread around itself a few times before passing it through the loop. Finish the knot with another overhand knot and pull tight (figure 3).

Navajo Canyon,
page 44

fig. 1

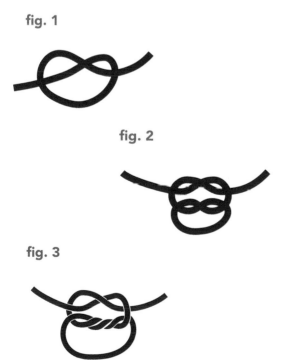

fig. 2

fig. 3

touch of the ivory coast

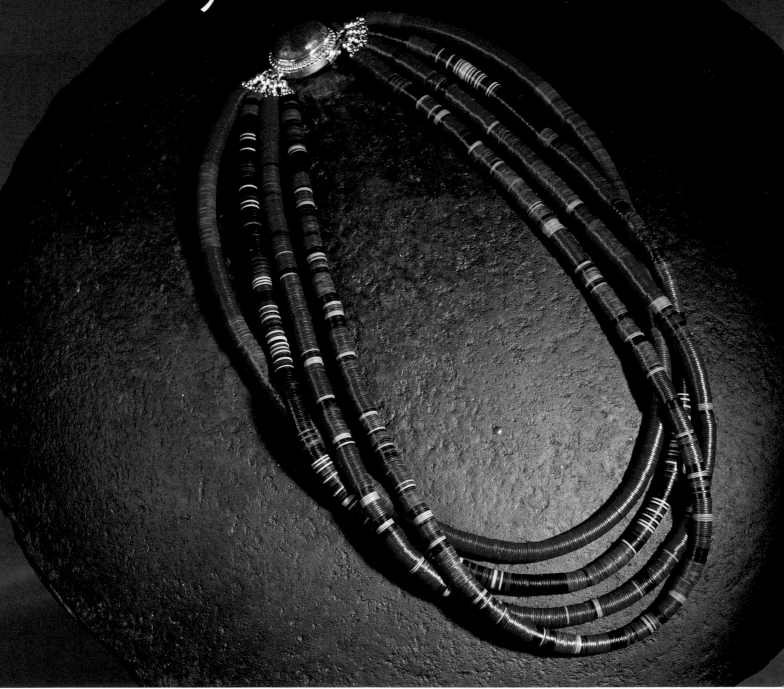

Four separate strands of mostly red African heishi beads make a stunning statement around your neck. Wear it on a tour of the African coast or a tour of your neighborhood haunts.

Designer: Sherry Duquet

Finished Size

18 inches (45.7 cm) long

Materials

4,000 African heishi trade beads, approximately 50 per inch (2.5 cm)

4 lengths of 0.014-inch (0.4 mm) fine beading wire, each 24 inches (61 cm) long

8 sterling silver round decorative beads, 4 mm

8 sterling silver round finishing beads, 3 mm

8 sterling silver crimp tubes, 2 x 2 mm

1 sterling silver and gemstone two-strand box clasp

8 sterling silver crimp covers, 3 mm

Tools

Ruler or tape measure

Beading board

Crimping pliers

Bevel cutters

Flat-nose pliers

Instructions

1. On the beading board, slide one of the 24-inch (61 cm) lengths of beading wire gently through the trade beads while they're still on the twine, pushing the trade beads onto the wire a few inches at a time. You'll want to thread beads from the different-colored original strands to create the desired color combination.

2. Next, place one 4-mm decorative bead, one 3-mm finishing bead, and one crimp tube on the end of the strand. Thread the wire through one of the loops on one side of the box clasp. Next, feed the wire back through the crimp tube, the finishing bead, the decorative bead, and several of the trade beads. Pull the wire snugly, but not too tightly, against the clasp. Using the crimping pliers, crimp the crimp tube firmly around the wire. Trim any excess wire with the bevel cutters. Repeat this step on the other end of the strand, attaching that end to a corresponding loop on the other side of the box clasp.

3. Repeat steps 1 and 2 for each of the other three strands. (Two strands will be attached to each loop of the clasp.)

4. Using the flat-nose pliers, close the crimp covers around the crimp tubes on all four strands.

hill tribe stunner

The silver beads, toggle, and fish pendant crafted by the Karen Hill Tribe of northern Thailand are a perfect match for pale blue stone rondelles. The fish swims across your neckline, while the blue beads cascade above like air bubbles.

Instructions

Designer: Catherine Hodge

Finished Size

18 inches (45.7 cm) long

Materials

16-inch (40 cm) strand of graduated Blue Quartz stone rondelles, ranging from approximately 8 mm x 10 mm to 16 mm x 20 mm. (The strand should have about 35 rondelles; the project uses 30 of them.)

24-inch (60 cm) length of 0.019-inch (0.5 mm) beading wire

4 crimps, 2 x 2 mm

Karen Hill Tribe silver toggle clasp, approximately 1½ inches (3.8 cm) wide

4 silver crimp covers

14 Karen Hill Tribe silver barrel beads, 6 mm

2 Karen Hill Tribe silver nautilus beads, 12 mm

Karen Hill Tribe silver fish pendant, approximately 2½ x 2¾ inches (6.4 x 7 cm)

Tools

Beading board

Crimping pliers

Wire cutters

1. Carefully cut the strand of rondelles and place them on a beading board in the order that they were strung, with the largest bead in the center. If there are an odd number of beads, remove the center one and place it to the side. Remove the smallest bead from each end of the strand in pairs until 30 beads remain.

2. On the beading wire, string a crimp, the smallest rondelle from one end of the board, another crimp, and the next rondelle. (Throughout the rest of the project, continue using rondelles in order from this end of the board.) Thread the toggle bar onto the wire.

3. Thread the end of the wire back through the rondelles and crimps. Use the crimping pliers to first close the crimps, and then to gently close a crimp cover over each crimp. Trim the wire tail close to the crimp.

4. String the next seven rondelles from the board. String a barrel bead and a rondelle. Repeat three times. Then string a nautilus bead and a rondelle, followed by a barrel bead and a rondelle.

5. String three barrel beads, the pendant, and another barrel bead. The goal is to use enough barrel beads on each side of the bail to cover to the outer edge of the pendant. The next rondelle strung should rest beside the pendant, rather than behind it (figure 1). If necessary, adjust the number of barrel beads used in this step.

fig. 1

6. String a rondelle, a barrel bead, a rondelle, and a nautilus bead. Check the symmetry of the necklace, as the beads should be a mirror image on each side of the pendant.

7. String a rondelle followed by a barrel bead. Repeat three times. String seven more rondelles. String a crimp bead and a rondelle. Repeat.

8. Thread the toggle clasp onto the wire. Thread the wire back through the first two rondelles and the crimp beads. Use your crimp pliers to close the crimps and add crimp covers, as in step 3. Trim any excess wire. If you have a short tail left, tuck it into the next rondelle.

bone and sinew earrings

Sinews work to hold bones together, and these African-inspired earrings make a strong statement all their own.

Instructions

1. Use the scissors to cut the sinew into two equal pieces, approximately 9 inches (22.9 cm) long. For the first earring, make a lark's head knot (figure 1), and loop one of the pieces of sinew around a bone ring. Pull snugly.

2. Loop the ring onto two long pins pushed into the foam board, as in macramé. Next, split the sinew into four strands. Using the tweezers or another pin can help with this.

3. String beads on each of the center two threads in the following order:
   • Striped 8/0
   • Red seed bead
   • Striped 8/0

4. String the center two threads through a 7-mm chevron bead.

5. String beads on each of the center two threads in the following order:
   • Striped 8/0 bead
   • Red seed bead
   • Striped 8/0 bead
   • Red seed bead
   • Striped 8/0 bead

6. String beads on each of the outer two threads in the following order:
   • Striped 8/0 bead
   • Red seed bead
   • Striped 8/0 bead
   • Three striped 6/0 beads
   • Striped 8/0 bead
   • Red seed bead
   • Striped 8/0 bead

7. String the left two threads through a 7-mm chevron bead, and then the right two threads through a 7-mm chevron bead.

Designer: Andrea L. Stern

Finished Size

Each: 6 inches (15.2 cm) long

Materials

18 inches (45.7 cm) of artificial sinew

2 bone rings, 16 mm

1 strand brown/white/black striped seed beads, size 8/0

1 strand red seed beads, size 8/0

8 chevron beads, 7 mm

24 striped beads, size 6/0

2 silver bails

2 head pins, 3 inches (7.6 cm) long

2 ear wires

Tools

Scissors

Ruler or tape measure

2 or 3 long pins

Scrap of foam board

Tweezers

Round-nose pliers

Wire cutters

fig. 1

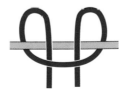

8. String beads on each of the center two threads in the following order:
    - Striped 8/0 bead
    - Red seed bead
    - Striped 8/0 bead
    - Three striped 6/0 beads
    - Striped 8/0 bead
    - Red seed bead
    - Striped 8/0 bead

    String both of the center two threads through a 7-mm chevron bead, then through a striped 8/0 bead. Tie a knot in the sinew.

9. String beads on each of the outer two threads in the following order:
    - *Striped 8/0 bead
    - Red seed bead

    Repeat from * five more times, ending with a striped 8/0 bead. Tie a knot in each outer thread.

10. Use the tweezers to split the sinew until it looks fringy. Trim as close or far away from the last bead as you'd like.

11. Repeat steps 1 through 10 for the second earring.

12. Attach the silver bails to the top of each bone ring.

13. Make the dangles by stringing a red seed bead, a 7-mm chevron, and another red seed bead onto a head pin. Use the round-nose pliers to bend the wire ¼ inch (6 mm) from the top at a 90° angle and make a simple loop. Push beads up to the loop, and bend the bottom wire 90°. Use the wire cutters to trim to ¼ inch (6 mm), and then make a second loop.

14. Repeat step 13 to make the second dangle.

15. Open both head pin loops and attach one loop to the top of the bail and the other to the ear wire. Repeat on the second earring.

source of the nile

Hand-painted wooden tube beads are interesting enough on their own. When you combine a hundred into one bracelet, though, the color and design variations make the whole a lot more than the sum of its parts.

source of the nile

Designer: Francie Broadie

Finished Size

7¼ inches (18.4 cm) clasped, 1¾ inches (4.4 cm) wide

Materials

Polyethylene beading cord, 6-pound test weight, or nylon beading cord, size D

Wax

87 to 100 painted wooden tube beads, 12 x 5 mm

60 to 75 silver-lined root beer AB seed beads, size 8/0

2 grams matte brown seed beads, size 11/0

2 wooden buttons, each ¾ inch (1.9 cm)

Tools

Ruler or tape measure

Scissors

Wax

Long beading needle, size 10

Brown marker (optional)

1. Use scissors to cut a 3-yard (2.7 m) length of polyethylene cord. If using nylon beading cord, cut a 6-yard (5.5 m) length; you'll work with this doubled. After waxing the cord, thread the needle.

2. String on four wooden tube beads, leaving an 8-inch (20.3 cm) tail. Turn the needle and pass through the second and first beads back toward the tail thread. The working thread should now be coming out of the same bead as the tail thread.

3. Working away from the tail thread, pick up one tube bead and pass the needle through the center bead and the bead on the left-hand side of the top row (figure 1). To get in position to add the next bead, bring the needle down through the bead on the top row that's to the right of the bead the working thread is exiting.

fig. 1

4. Pick up one bead and pass the needle down through the bead on the right on the bottom row.

5. Pick up a bead and pass up through the center bead and the second bead from the right on the top row. Turn and pass through the bead farthest to the right from top to bottom. Pick up a bead, and pass through the bead farthest to the right on the bottom row.

6. Pick up a bead and pass through the center bead and the bead farthest to the right on the top row, from bottom to top. Continue adding beads in this manner, alternating the turns. Work until the bracelet is the desired length, allowing about an inch for the clasp.

7. To embellish the bracelet, bring the thread so that it is exiting the bead on the end, heading away from the bracelet. Pick up one 8/0 bead, five 11/0 beads, and one 8/0 bead. Pass the needle down the tube bead to the left. Bring the needle up through the bead to the left of the one that the thread is exiting. Repeat for the length of both sides of the bracelet.

8. For the clasp, create the button end first. With thread exiting an edge bead at the end of the bracelet, pick up seven 11/0 beads, one 8/0, three 11/0 beads, the button, and seven 11/0 beads.

9. Pass back through the 8/0 bead, heading toward the body of the bracelet (figure 2). Pick up seven 11/0 beads and pass the needle through the opposite side of the tube bead on the end of the bracelet. Reinforce this thread path at least two more times.

fig. 2

10. Repeat steps 8 and 9 for the second button on the other edge bead at the same end of the bracelet.

11. To make the loops, you may need to tie on a new thread at the opposite end of the bracelet. Bring the thread out one of the edge beads at the end of the bracelet.

12. Pick up five 11/0 beads, one 8/0, and enough 11/0 beads to go around your button. Pass back through the 8/0 bead, heading toward the body of the bracelet. Pick up five more 11/0 beads, and pass through the tube bead from the opposite side.

13. Reinforce this thread path at least two more times. Remember the loop will tighten up with the reinforcement. It's better for the loop to be a bit too loose than too tight. You can always embellish the loop to tighten it up if necessary, but you can't make it bigger.

14. Repeat steps 11 through 13 for the second loop.

15. Tie off the thread, making three or four half-hitches in different locations. Trim the thread close to the work. If desired, touch up any thread that shows with the brown marker.

turquoise mosaic

Thai and Balinese beads are joined in this beautiful necklace, and a clever clasp links the moon and a star.

Instructions

1. Use the scissors to cut a 24-inch (61 cm) length of the beading thread, and then pull it tightly to stretch it out. (If you skip this step, the weight of the pendant will eventually cause your necklace to stretch.)

2. Thread the pendant onto the thread, centering it so that you now have two threads on which to bead.

3. Thread beads onto each thread in the following order:
   - Small Bali silver bead
   - Ceramic bead
   - Medium Thai silver rondelle bead
   - Barrel bead
   - Bone bead
   - Barrel bead
   - Ceramic bead
   - Larger Thai silver rondelle bead
   - Mosaic round bead
   - Larger Thai silver rondelle bead
   - Ceramic bead
   - Barrel bead
   - Bone bead
   - Barrel bead
   - Ceramic bead
   - Medium Thai silver rondelle bead
   - Ceramic bead
   - Thai silver tube bead

4. Fill the rest of the strand as follows:
   - *3 ceramic beads
   - 1 silver cuff bead

   Repeat from * four more times; then string 12 ceramic beads.

5. String the thread through the hole in the bead tip. Using the tweezers, make a knot and pull tight to gather the knot as close to the bead tip as possible. Repeat on the other side. Glue the knots with the bead tip cement or nail polish. Let dry and then trim.

6. Using the flat-nose pliers, close the bead tip. Put the loop of the bead tip through the loop on the clasp and close the loop. Repeat on the other side.

Designer: Andrea L. Stern

Finished Size

21 inches (53.3 cm) long

Materials

Nylon beading thread, size FFF or comparable

Turquoise inlay mosaic pendant, 30 mm

2 small Bali silver beads

64 ceramic beads, 5 mm

4 medium Thai silver rondelle beads

8 barrel beads, 6 mm

4 round bone beads, 10 mm

4 larger Thai silver rondelle beads

2 round turquoise inlay mosaic beads, 15 mm

2 Thai silver tube beads, 10 mm

10 silver cuff beads, 7 mm

Bead tips

Bead tip cement or nail polish

Toggle clasp

Tools

Scissors

Ruler or tape measure

Tweezers

Flat-nose pliers

wrapped leather cuff

A tightly woven leather cord snugly grasps your wrist on one side of this cuff, and it holds tight to a bead array of your choice on the other.

Instructions

1. Wrap the silver wire in a tidy coil around one end of your cuff bracelet until it's secure, approximately six or seven times. First, plan your design, and then string the beads onto the wire. Stretch the wire across the top of the two bars of the cuff, and arrange the beads so there is a slight amount of breathing space between each one.

2. Wrap wire around the opposite side of the bracelet to hold it in place. Use the wire cutters to cut the wire, leaving just enough so that you can make any necessary adjustments.

3. Make sure you're satisfied with the bead arrangement before you start weaving with the leather. Tie the leather cord in a snug knot at the point where you started the wire, just below where the cuff splits into two bars. Begin weaving the cord back and forth between the two bars and under the beads in a figure-eight pattern. Secure the bead wire as you go by looping the leather cord around it once or twice between the beads and then continuing with the weaving pattern. Take care to keep consistent tension, and check placement of the beads often.

4. Tie the leather off as you did when you started and cut with the scissors. Add a drop or two of adhesive over your knots for extra security. Finish by adding a drop of adhesive on your wrapped wire coil and sliding (or screwing if it's a snug fit) your silver spacer bead into place. Repeat for the opposite side.

Designer's Tip

You can use a jeweler's saw to open up the cuff bracelet a little more. This will make it weaker initially, but the woven leather cord will reinforce it.

Designer: Candie Cooper

Finished Size

Approximately 8 inches (20.3 cm) around; adjustable

Materials

Split cuff bracelet

20-gauge silver craft wire

Assorted beads, including 5 focal beads and 4 glass spacer beads; size will vary depending on cuff bracelet size

Leather cord, 1.5 mm diameter

Multipurpose adhesive

2 silver spacer beads with large holes

Tools

Wire cutters

Scissors

Jeweler's saw (optional)

tiger's-eye tassel

"Where did you buy that necklace?" is what your friends will ask when you debut this exotic and beautiful piece. Keep them guessing.

Instructions

1. To make the pendant, begin by placing the statue and the large rectangle bead on the paper. Trace a line around them in the shape you want the final pendant to be. Be sure to leave room at the top for the jump ring to be inserted into the leather. Set the statue and bead aside.

2. Hold the paper up to the light, and then fold it in half vertically, matching up the traced lines. Use the scissors to cut on the line through the folded paper so that your shape is perfectly symmetrical when you open it up.

3. Place the pattern made above on one piece of the leather. Trace the shape onto the leather with a pen. Glue the statue and large rectangle bead onto the leather, placing them inside the traced lines. Allow the glue to dry.

4. Cut 2 yards (1.8 m) of the thread, and thread the needle. Sew both the rectangle bead and the statue down onto the leather, going through the leather several times. End by tying a knot in the back. Trim, leaving at least ½ inch (1.3 cm) beyond the knot.

5. Cut the leather on the line you previously traced. Be careful not to cut any of the threads you used to sew the statue and bead down.

6. Spread the glue on the back of the pendant form and place on the other piece of leather. Let dry. (If your leather is thin and too flexible, cut a piece from a milk carton or juice drink and place it in between the leather pieces for extra strength.)

Designer: Jamie Cloud Eakin

Finished Size

19½ inches (49.5 cm) long

Materials

Small statue, approximately ⅝ x 1¼ inches (1.6 x 3.2 cm)

Antique brown jade rectangle bead, 25 x 15 x 5 mm

2 pieces of leather, approximately 2 x 3 inches (5.1 x 7.6 cm)

Glue

Thread

Piece of a milk carton or juice box (optional)

18-gauge round jump ring, 8 mm

5-foot (1.5 m) length of 0.019-inch (0.5 mm) flexible beading wire

3-to-1 loop filigree finding

13 silver color crimp beads

149 tortoise color round beads, 4 mm

8 hollow metal rondelle beads, 6 x 8 mm

15 faceted round tiger's-eye beads, 8 mm

11 rectangle tiger's-eye beads, 8 x 10 mm

Hollow metal bead with a flat side

Hook-and-eye clasp

8 hollow metal beads in three or four different designs, ranging from 12 to 8 mm

Tools

Sheet of paper and pen

Scissors

Ruler or tape measure

Needle

Black permanent marker (optional)

Awl or sewing machine needle

2 chain-nose pliers

Wire cutters

Crimping pliers

11. Repeat step 10 for the other two pieces of wire.

12. Starting from the left dangling wire and working to the right, add beads to each wire in the following order:

- 17 round tortoise beads, metal rondelle, round tiger's-eye, round tortoise bead, crimp
- 18 round tortoise beads, metal rondelle, rectangle tiger's-eye, round tortoise bead, crimp
- 20 round tortoise beads, metal rondelle, rectangle tiger's-eye, round tortoise bead, crimp
- 19 round tortoise beads, metal rondelle, round tiger's-eye, round tortoise bead, crimp
  - 17 round tortoise beads, metal rondelle, rectangle tiger's-eye, round tortoise bead, crimp
    - 16 round tortoise beads, metal rondelle, round tiger's-eye, round tortoise bead, crimp

Push the beads up to the top but do not push too tight; leave some flexibility in the strand. Crimp the crimp bead. Trim the wire near the crimp bead.

13. Cut 9 inches (22.9 cm) of the flexible beading wire. Add a crimp bead on one end and pass the wire through one of the side loops on the top of the finding. Pass one end of the wire back through the crimp bead, taking care to leave just enough length so the wire can pass through one round tortoise bead. Push the crimp bead up to the finding so it's snug, but not too snug. Crimp.

7. When the glue from step 6 is dry, trim around the second piece of leather to match the first leather piece.

Designer's Tip

After step 7, you can use a black permanent marker to paint the edge of the glued leather pieces. This gives a nice outline to your pendant.

8. Use an awl or thick pin (a sewing machine needle works well), and pierce a hole in the top of the pendant. Use the chain-nose pliers to open the jump ring, insert it into the hole, and close the ring.

9. To make the tassel, begin by using the wire cutters to cut three 10-inch (25.4 cm) pieces of flexible wire.

10. Fold one piece of the wire in half, and then thread through the bottom loop of the finding. Thread a crimp bead through both ends of the wire, and push the bead up near the finding. Use the crimping pliers to crimp.

14. Add five round tortoise beads to the long end of the wire. Pass the short end of the wire through the first round tortoise bead, and trim the short end close to the crimp bead. Now pass the long end of the wire through the rectangle bead on the pendant.

15. Pick up one round tortoise bead, the flat hollow metal bead, and one round tortoise bead. Pass the wire through the rectangle bead again.

16. Pick up five round tortoise beads and one crimp bead. Loop the wire through the other side hole on the top of the finding, and then pass the wire back through the crimp bead and one round tortoise bead. Pull to adjust the tension. Crimp the crimp bead, and trim near the crimp (figure 1).

fig. 1

17. To string the necklace, begin by cutting 20 inches (50.8 cm) of flexible wire. Add a crimp bead on one end, and loop through the hook clasp. Crimp the crimp bead, and trim near the crimp.

18. String on the beads. Start with one round tortoise bead, and then pick up the next bead in the following list and then another round tortoise bead. Repeat from the list, adding one round tortoise bead between each bead in the list. End with a round tiger's-eye bead.
- Round tiger's-eye
- Hollow metal rondelle
- Round tiger's-eye
- Tiger's-eye rectangle
- Hollow metal bead
- Round tiger's-eye
- Tiger's-eye rectangle
- Hollow metal bead
- Round tiger's-eye
- Tiger's-eye rectangle
- Round tiger's-eye
- Hollow metal bead
- Tiger's-eye rectangle
- Hollow metal rondelle
- Round tiger's-eye

String through the jump ring on the pendant.

19. Repeat step 18 in reverse order.

20. Add one crimp bead and the eye of the clasp. String back through the crimp bead plus one round tortoise bead. Pull to adjust the tension and crimp the crimp bead. Trim the wire.

red-hot cinnabar

Cinnabar is derived
from the same ore that
produces mercury.
Make this necklace
and turn up the heat.

Instructions

1. Use the wire cutters to cut a 24-inch (61 cm) length of beading wire and string the focal bead.

2. First, plan your design, and then, working from the focal bead outward, begin to add beads to each side of the necklace until you've reached your desired length. Be careful not to let the beads slip off the end of the thread. Use an alligator clip or a small piece of tape at one end, if desired.

3. String on a crimp bead, a ¾-inch (1.9 cm) length of French wire, and half of the clasp.

4. Bring the end of the wire back through the crimp bead and a few of the beads on the necklace. Make sure the French wire does not slip into the crimp bead (figure 1). Adjust the end of the wire so that the French wire does not bunch up.

fig. 1

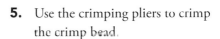

5. Use the crimping pliers to crimp the crimp bead.

6. Repeat steps 3 to 5 on the other side of the necklace, making sure you don't have any excess wire showing.

7. Use the wire cutters to trim the ends of the wire close to the necklace.

8. Add the crimp covers. Hold the cover in the round outer notch of the crimping tool, with the cover opening face out. Align each cover over a crimp bead and gently squeeze. You may have to turn the necklace slightly and squeeze the crimp cover a second time to get it to close completely. The goal is to have a nice round cover when you're finished.

Designer: Francie Broadie

Finished Size

17¾ inches (45.1 cm) long

Materials

24-inch (61 cm) length of 0.019-inch (0.5 mm) beading wire

Round red-and-black cinnabar disc focal bead, 36 mm

20 matte black glass melon-shaped rondelles, 9 x 5 mm

16 carved bone spacer beads

4 hexagonal black cinnabar beads, 18 mm

2 triangular red cinnabar beads, 30 mm long

2 black round carved horn beads, 16 mm

4 red round cinnabar beads, 15 mm

2 crimp beads

2 pieces of French wire, each ¾-inch (1.9 cm) long

Sterling silver clasp

2 sterling silver crimp covers

Tools

Wire cutters

Ruler or measuring tape

Alligator clip or small piece of tape (optional)

Crimping pliers

Kenya is a common source for batik bones, which are combined here with a variety of intriguing brass beads.

cow bone necklace

Instructions

1. Straighten the wire with nylon pliers, if necessary.

2. Feed the medium brass bead onto the wire. Create a simple loop at one end of the wire, using your chain-nose and round-nose pliers. Slide the bead so that it's flush against the loop. Create a loop on the other side of the bead (figure 1). Cut the wire with a flush or side wire cutter. Use the chain-nose pliers to adjust the loops so they are tight against the bead. File wire ends smooth where needed.

   fig. 1

3. Repeat step 2, connecting your new loop to the last one you made. This time feed five batik bone beads onto the wire, bending the wire so that the five beads are slightly arced.

4. Repeat the process described in step 2, stringing the beads in the following order:
   • Three batik bone beads
   • Medium brass bead
   • Large batik bone bead
   • Five batik bone beads (Remember to bend the wire so the beads are slightly arced.)
   • Large brass bead
   • Five batik bone beads (Remember to bend the wire so the beads are slightly arced.)
   • Three batik bone beads
   • Small brass bead
   • Large brass bead
   • Three batik bone beads
   • Large brass bead
   • Large batik bone bead
   • Three batik bone beads

5. Attach the pieces of the clasp to both ends of the necklace.

Designers: Elizabeth Glass Geltman and Rachel Geltman

Finished Size

22 inches (55.9 cm) long

Materials

16-gauge brass round wire

2 small brass beads

32 assorted batik bone beads

1 medium brass bead

2 large batik bone beads

3 large brass beads

Clasp

Tools

Nylon pliers

Chain-nose pliers

Round-nose pliers

Flush or side wire cutters

Needle file or cup burr

Mandrel or small marker (optional)

Steel bench block or anvil (optional)

Rawhide, plastic, or chasing hammer (optional)

Designer's Tip

Metals are expensive. To avoid loss when creating jewelry, don't cut a length of wire and then trim the excess. Instead, work directly from the wire spool and then cut the wire to the exact fit.

navajo canyon

Knotted khaki linen laces
beads around your neck,
with a delicate jangle of
beads hanging below.

Instructions

1. Measure and then use the scissors to cut four lengths of the waxed linen, each length 2 yards (1.8 m) long.

2. Line up the strands. Find the center of the stack of linen threads. Tie an overhand knot 1¼ inches (3.2 cm) from the center. To tie an overhand knot, make a loop with all of the threads and pull the rest of the threads through the loop (figure 1). Tie a second knot on the other side of the necklace 1¼ inches (3.2 cm) from the center.

fig. 1

3. Pin one of the knots to the macramé board or the pillow. Arrange the linen threads so that there is one strand to the left, two held together in the center, and one strand to the right.

4. Loosely braid the strands together. Continue braiding until the braided part measures 4½ to 5 inches (11.4 to 12.7 cm). Tie an overhand knot at the end of the braided section.

5. Repeat steps 3 and 4 on the other side of the necklace, making sure you divide the strands as in step 3.

6. On one side of the necklace, thread one turquoise spacer bead through the two center strands. While holding the left and right threads to the outside edges of the bead, split the two center strands apart and tie all four strands into a square knot. To tie a square knot, loop one thread over the other as you would when you begin tying your shoes. Pull it close against the bead, making sure that the outside threads are still on opposite sides of the bead. Loop the thread one more time in the same way to complete the knot.

Designer: Francie Broadie

Finished Size

23 inches (58.4 cm) long, plus a 4½-inch (11.4 cm) tassel

Materials

4 lengths of 2-ply waxed khaki linen, each 2 yards (1.8 m) long

7 turquoise spacer beads, 10 mm

7 metal round rose beads, 6 mm

4 carved bone beads with a large hole, 12 mm

26 matte copper seed beads, size 6/0

2 turquoise glass crow beads

Carved turquoise rondelle with hole large enough to fit eight strands of the cord, 18 mm

3 round turquoise beads, 8 mm

4 round turquoise beads, 6 mm

3 bone-colored beads, 4 mm

Tools

Ruler or tape measure

Scissors

T-pin or safety pin

Macramé board or pillow

Designer's Tip

A macramé board will have illustrations of the basic knots, something that is often quite helpful.

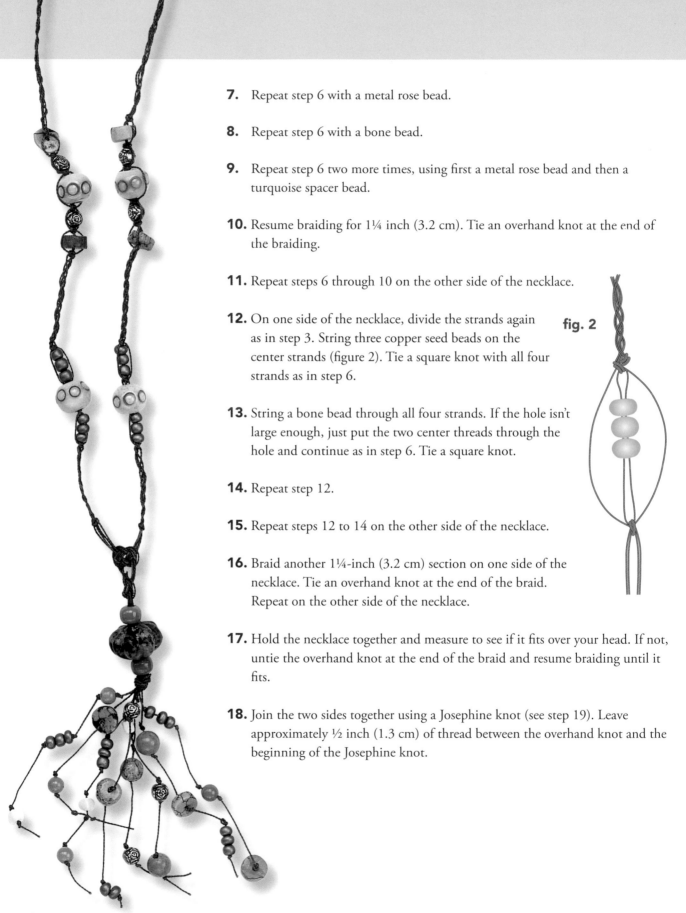

7. Repeat step 6 with a metal rose bead.

8. Repeat step 6 with a bone bead.

9. Repeat step 6 two more times, using first a metal rose bead and then a turquoise spacer bead.

10. Resume braiding for 1¼ inch (3.2 cm). Tie an overhand knot at the end of the braiding.

11. Repeat steps 6 through 10 on the other side of the necklace.

12. On one side of the necklace, divide the strands again as in step 3. String three copper seed beads on the center strands (figure 2). Tie a square knot with all four strands as in step 6.

fig. 2

13. String a bone bead through all four strands. If the hole isn't large enough, just put the two center threads through the hole and continue as in step 6. Tie a square knot.

14. Repeat step 12.

15. Repeat steps 12 to 14 on the other side of the necklace.

16. Braid another 1¼-inch (3.2 cm) section on one side of the necklace. Tie an overhand knot at the end of the braid. Repeat on the other side of the necklace.

17. Hold the necklace together and measure to see if it fits over your head. If not, untie the overhand knot at the end of the braid and resume braiding until it fits.

18. Join the two sides together using a Josephine knot (see step 19). Leave approximately ½ inch (1.3 cm) of thread between the overhand knot and the beginning of the Josephine knot.

19. To make the Josephine knot, make a loop with the left-hand thread so that the threads closest to the braiding are on the bottom and the rest of the thread rests on the top of the loop. Lay this loop on top of the right-hand threads. Bring the working threads on the right-hand side over the bottom strands and under the top strands. Feed these same threads down through the first loop, staying on the top side of the right-hand threads that are closest to the necklace. Now bring these same threads up underneath the center threads and out of the loop (figure 3). Gently tug on all four bunches of thread to tighten the knot. You may have to adjust it a bit to get all of the threads to lie flat.

fig. 3

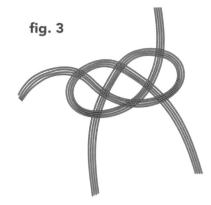

20. Make a second Josephine knot below the first one, leaving a bit of space between the two knots.

21. Holding all eight strands together, string a crow bead, the large turquoise rondelle, and another crow bead.

22. Tie an overhand knot with all of the strands held together.

23. To make the tassel fringe, tie an overhand knot on one of the strands, and string one of your remaining beads. Push the bead up to the knot, then tie another overhand knot directly below the bead. Add anywhere from two to five of the remaining beads to each of the eight strands in this manner, keeping them no farther than 3½ inches (8.9 cm) away from the big overhand knot in the center. Stagger the bead placement to create a nice full tassel.

24. Trim each thread to approximately 3½ inches (8.9 cm) from the center overhand knot. Basically, you want the tassel to be even. Measure your longest fringe and cut the rest of them to the same length.

Designer's Tip

This necklace has no clasp, so make sure that it will fit over your head before you join the two sides together. If it doesn't, extend the braid a bit at the end of the last set of beads. There's enough thread to allow for a few inches of adjustment.

golden dunes bracelet

Like an iridescent pearl spotted on a sandy beach, this bracelet is an unexpected delight to keep and treasure.

Designer: Elizabeth Larsen

Finished Size

8 inches (20.3 cm) long

Materials

20-gauge full hard or half hard gold-filled wire, 7 ft. (2.1 m)

96 round strawberry conch shell beads, 5 mm

14 gold spacer rings

24-gauge (full hard or half hard) gold-filled wire, 22 ft. (6.7 m)

Cement adhesive for nonporous surfaces

10 coin golden-lip shells, 15 mm

19 coin brown-lip shells, 10 mm

9 medium freeform mother-of-pearl nuggets

Tools

Tape measure

1 knitting needle (for jump rings), size 2 US (2.75 mm)

Wire cutters

2 needle-nose pliers

Round-nose pliers

Instructions

1. Make the base chain. First, create your own jump rings as follows. Cut a 6-foot length (1.8 m) of the 20-gauge gold-filled wire and wind it tightly in a coil around the knitting needle. (You'll need 118 jump rings altogether.) Slide the coil off the needle, and spread the rings slightly to make them easier to cut. Cut one ring off with the flush side of the wire cutters, then flip the cutters to cut the other wire tip of the ring flush. Continue with the other rings in the coil. Link the jump rings in pairs, using the two needle-nose pliers to make a 6½-inch (16.5 cm) chain. (Later you'll attach each half of the toggle clasp to the chain with the extra jump rings.)

2. Next, start to make the ring of the toggle clasp. Use the wire cutters to cut a 3½-inch (8.9 cm) piece of 20-gauge gold-filled wire, and then make a simple loop at one end with the round-nose pliers.

3. Add 11 of the round strawberry conch shell beads, with one gold spacer ring in between each shell. Curve the wire into a ring, making sure the beads are spaced far enough apart so that the wire can bend into a circle. Close with a second simple loop, and rotate the ends so they are parallel to each other. Connect the two ends together with a jump ring.

4. To make the bar of the clasp, measure and cut a 1¾-inch (4.4 cm) piece of 20-gauge gold-filled wire, and create a simple loop at one end. Add three conch shell beads and two gold spacers, interspersing the spacers between the beads.

Designer's Tip

If you would prefer not to make your own jump rings as described in step 1, you can instead go to a jewelry-supply store or catalog and purchase 20-gauge gold-filled jump rings with an interior diameter of 3 mm or slightly less. If you do, you will only need a 1-foot (30.5 cm) length of gold-filled wire to make the project.

5. Take an extra piece of 20-gauge gold-filled wire and create a small figure eight (i.e., two simple loops). Add the figure eight to the toggle bar, and then slide three additional conch shell beads onto the bar, with gold spacers between them as in step 4. Close off the bar with another simple loop. Attach the figure eight to the end of the base chain with a jump ring (figure 1).

fig. 1

6. To prepare all of the beads for assembly, start by cutting a 2-inch (5.1 cm) to 2½-inch (6.4 cm) piece of 24-gauge gold-filled wire. (The larger shells may need the larger piece of wire.) Using the round-nose pliers, form a simple loop at one end. Add one of the beads to the wire. Secure the wire end and bead with a dab of glue. Repeat this step for each bead.

7. To construct the bracelet, lay out the beads in the following order:
- *3 strawberry conch shell beads
- Golden-lip shell
- Brown-lip shell
- Strawberry conch shells
- Mother-of-pearl nugget
- Brown-lip shell

Repeat from * with the remaining beads.

8. Start at one end of the chain, and begin attaching the beads. Attach one bead to either side of a link set, using the wrapped loop technique. Continue adding beads in this fashion until you come to the end of the bracelet. Adjust the beads on each link so that there are not too many of the same beads on one side.

year of the dragon

Whatever your Chinese zodiac sign is, wearing this necklace will be a mark of good fortune.

year of the dragon

Designer: Jeannette Chiang Bardi

Finished Size

17½ inches (44.5 cm) long

Materials

30-inch (76.2 cm) length of 22-gauge square half hard gold-filled wire, either 12/20 or 14/20

5 round cream color (natural) river stone beads, 6 mm

5 round earth tones (natural) picture jasper beads, 6 mm

6 round gold Swarovski crystal pearls, 6 mm

5 round black Swarovski crystal pearls, 6 mm

3 diamond-shaped black imitation cinnabar beads, 15 mm

Antique brass Chinese Zodiac "protective talisman" coin drop, 30 x 23 mm

6-inch (15.2 cm) length of black leather cord, 2 mm

4 gold-filled or gold-plated coil ends, each 10.5 x 3 mm

Lobster clasp with ring, 12 x 5 x 2.5 mm

Tools

Ruler or tape measure

Wire cutters

Round-nose pliers

Flat-nose pliers

Scissors

Instructions

1. To make the bead/wire components, begin by cutting the gold-filled wire with the wire cutters into twenty-three 1-inch (2.5 cm) lengths and three 1½-inch (3.8 cm) lengths.

2. Take one of the 1-inch (2.5 cm) lengths of gold-filled wire, and using the round-nose pliers, bend ⅓ inch (8.5 mm) of the wire into a simple loop. Slip a 6-mm bead on the straight end of the wire. With the bead snug to the first loop, create a second loop on the other end of the bead, but leave the loop slightly open (see the steps in figure 1). Create a total of 21 bead/wire components out of the 6-mm beads, using the 1-inch (2.5 cm) lengths of gold-filled wire.

fig. 1

3. Using the same procedure as used when making the 6 mm bead/wire components, use the three 1½ inch (3.8 cm) lengths of gold-filled wire to create three cinnabar bead/wire components. Bend ½ inch (1.3 cm) of the wire for each loop on either side of the bead.

4. Set aside one gold pearl/wire component and one cinnabar bead/wire component to be used for the pendant.

5. With the remaining bead/wire components, create two 11-bead strands by linking together the 6-mm bead/wire components made in steps 2 and 3, using the flat-nose pliers to close each link securely. Alternate the bead types, and attach a cinnabar bead as the ninth bead/wire component in each strand. This will make the two sides of the necklace.

6. To create the pendant, begin by linking the remaining gold pearl/wire component to one end of the remaining cinnabar bead. On the other side of the gold pearl/wire component, link the Chinese coin.

7. Bring the ends of the two necklace strands together, with the cinnabar beads toward the bottom, and attach the bottom two links together with the cinnabar end of the pendant.

8. To make and connect the cord ends, begin by cutting two 3-inch (7.6 cm) lengths of leather cord.

9. Bend both ends of each cord back ½ inch (1.3 cm). Use the flat-nose pliers to squeeze the folded end so that it will keep its shape and slip more easily into a coil end, leaving a leather loop. Twist gently to insert the coil end over the leather loop (top of figure 2). Secure the coil by squeezing the first and last loop of the coil onto the cord, again using the flat-nose pliers (bottom of figure 2). Repeat for the other three ends.

fig. 2

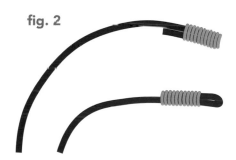

10. Use the remaining two 1-inch (2.5 cm) lengths of gold-filled wire to create two links, using the same procedure referenced in step 2 (only without the beads). Slip the open end of one of the links through the leather loop at the end of each cord and close to secure. Attach half of the lobster claw clasp to one of the links. Attach the lobster claw ring to a link on the other cord. Finally, link the necklace to the other ends of the cords.

tears of shiva

The Rudraksha tree, which grows from the Ganges River to the Himalayan foothills, yields the Rishi seeds featured in this Indian-inspired set.

Instructions

Finished Size

Necklace: 21 inches (53.3 cm) long

Earrings: 2 inches (5.1 cm) long

Materials

2 feet (61 cm) of 0.019-inch (0.5 mm) beading wire

2 crimp beads

Decorative hook-and-eye clasp

8 seed beads, size 6/0

10 burned wood ovals, 15 mm

16 brass cuff beads

14 ceramic discs, 10 mm

14 Rishi seeds

9 carved bone rounds, 15 mm

2 head pins

2 ear wires

Tools

Crimping pliers

Wire cutters

Round-nose pliers

Designer's Tip

The name of this project is inspired by an ancient story that the Rudraksha tree first appeared growing in ground watered by tears from the god Shiva. The tree's seeds are traditionally used to make strings of Hindu prayer beads.

1. Slide the wire through a crimp bead, through the holes of the first piece of the clasp, and then back through the crimp bead. Using the crimping pliers, close the crimp. Trim excess wire with the wire cutters.

2. String beads as follows:
   • 2 seed beads
   • *Wood oval
   • Brass cuff
   • Ceramic disc
   • Rishi seed
   • Carved bone
   • Rishi seed
   • Ceramic disc
   • Brass cuff
   Repeat from * six times, then end with a wood oval and two seed beads.

3. Repeat step 1 for the second piece of the clasp.

4. To make the earrings, slide on one seed bead, a carved bone bead, brass cuff, and wood oval onto a head pin. End with a second seed bead. Using the round-nose pliers, bend the head pin 90° and trim to ¼ inch (.6 cm). Then make a simple loop, attach the head pin to an ear wire, and close the loop. Repeat for the second earring.

peruvian prayer beads

It's not all about the looks. Sometimes—as with this strand of stone, metal, and bone—how it feels in your hands is just as important.

Instructions

1. Insert the sterling silver head pin through one each of the hematite, bone rondelle, and horn rondelle beads, plus two seed beads. Then use the chain-nose pliers to shape a loop at the end of the head pin, wrapping the wire around itself so the loop will remain in place. Next, cut an 18-inch (45.7 cm) length of waxed linen thread with the scissors, and attach it to the head pin loop by securely knotting it. It's best to tie two square knots and then use a toothpick to add a drop of glue to the knot centers to ensure that the thread doesn't come untied (figure 1).

2. Insert the linen thread and head pin into the focal bead. Then begin adding seed beads to the thread until the seed beads are flush with the end of the focal bead. The seed beads will stabilize the movement of the focal bead so it remains centered on the string.

3. String the remaining beads in this order: horn rondelle, *hematite, copper, hematite, inlaid yak bone. Repeat from * until the 10 yak bone meditation beads are in place. Finish by adding horn rondelle, bone rondelle, horn rondelle, and 19 seed beads.

4. Using both of the chain-nose pliers, open the jump ring and then add the token. Next, place the jump ring and token on the thread. Pull the thread back through the horn rondelle bead, making sure the string is tight, and tie a square knot. Insert the thread through the bone rondelle and horn rondelle beads and tie another square knot. Continue by pulling the thread through the first yak bone bead. Finally, add a touch of white glue to the centers of the knots, clip the thread, and the prayer beads are complete.

5. As an optional step, add an inlaid yak bone bead to each string of the velvet pouch, and you have an eye-catching way to carry your prayer beads with you.

Designer's Tip

If you experience problems threading the seed beads onto the linen thread, use sharp scissors to clip the end of the thread to a point, and the beads will go on easily.

fig. 1

Designer: Karen J. Lauseng

Finished Size

1 x 9½ inches (2.5 x 24.1 cm)

Materials

1-inch (2.5 cm) sterling silver head pin

21 hematite disc beads, 4 mm

2 natural bone rondelle beads, 6 mm

4 golden horn rondelle beads, 10 mm

Approximately 30 amber seed beads, size 11/0

18-inch (45.7 cm) strand of waxed linen thread

1 stone focal bead with a large center hole, approximately 1 x ½ inches (2.5 x 1.3 cm) long

10 copper disc beads, 4 mm

12 inlaid yak bone beads from Peru

Jump ring

1 token, approximately 1 x 1¼ inches (2.5 x 3.2 cm) long

4½-inch square (11.4 cm) velvet pouch (optional)

Tools

2 sets of chain-nose pliers

Ruler or tape measure

Sharp scissors

Toothpick

White craft glue

trade caravan

Simple wire loop and jump ring techniques create a necklace
well worth trading for.

Instructions

Designer: Karen J. Lauseng

Finished Size

18 inches (45.7 cm) long

Materials

Strong black tea or coffee

9 bone hairpipe beads, 1 inch
(2.5 cm) long

50-inch (127 cm) length of 18-gauge sterling
silver round wire

17 random-shaped brass disc beads, 8 mm

9 brass rondelle beads, 8 mm

9 horn rondelle beads, 8 mm

9 skunk Venetian trade beads, 14 mm

21 red-colored African white heart beads,
approximately 8 mm

16 brass spacer beads, 4 mm

8 black frosted-glass beads, 10 mm

150 18-gauge sterling jump rings,
3 mm

Purchased clasp

Tools

Cup

Flush cutters

Ruler or tape measure

Fine-tooth flat jeweler's file

Round-nose pliers

2 chain-nose pliers

1. Antique the bone beads by dropping them into a cup of very strong black tea and letting them soak for about a half hour. Check on them often, and remove them when they've reached the desired shade.

2. Use the flush cutters to cut nine 3¼-inch (8.3 cm) lengths of 18-gauge sterling silver wire. File the ends of the wires flat with the jeweler's file.

3. Using your round-nose pliers, form a loop at one end of the wire. Next, add the beads to the wire in the following order:
   • Random-shaped brass disc bead
   • Bone hairpipe bead
   • Brass rondelle
   • Horn rondelle
   • Skunk bead
   • Red-colored white heart bead
   • Brass spacer bead
   When all the beads are in place, use the round-nose pliers to form a loop on the other end of the wire. Repeat this process until you have added beads to all nine sections of the silver wire. This collection of beads will be called Bead Group A (see the process shown in figure 1).

fig. 1

4. Cut eight 1¼-inch (3.2 cm) lengths of 18-gauge sterling silver wire. Prepare the wire as in step 3, and then add the beads in the following order:
• Brass spacer bead
• Red-colored white heart bead
• Brass spacer bead
Form the closing loop, and repeat the process until you have eight sets. This collection will be called Bead Group B.

5. Cut four 1¾-inch (4.4 cm) lengths of 18-gauge sterling silver wire, and prepare the wire in the same manner as in step 3. Add the beads in the following order:
• Black frosted-glass bead
• Random-shaped brass disc bead
• Red-colored white heart bead
• Random-shaped brass disc bead
• Black frosted-glass bead
Form the closing loop, and repeat the process until you have four sets. This collection will be called Bead Group C.

6. Now connect the sections together. Using the two sets of chain-nose pliers, open a jump ring. Slide on one bead set from Group A and one from Group B. Close the jump ring. Use another jump ring to add another Group A set to the other end of the connected Group B set. Continue adding jump rings and bead sets until all of the Group A beads are connected to Group B beads as shown in the main photo.

7. Using jump rings, attach two bead sets from Group C to each end of the chain. Adding an extra jump ring between these bead sets results in more uniform spacing.

8. When all the beads have been connected, continue adding jump rings on both ends of the necklace. The number of jump rings used will vary with the fit. A double chain looks really nice and balances the weight of the beads. Once you are satisfied with the fit, connect the jump rings to a purchased clasp.

Designer's Tip

"White heart beads" are just what their name implies: white at their heart and another color on the outside. The coloring agents used by early bead makers were often relatively expensive, so making trade beads of white glass and only coloring the surface was a more economical choice.

temple gate bracelet

Though this bracelet also contains
Chinese porcelain and Czech glass,
its exotic design and Thai silver beads
mark it as something you might
encounter in a Bangkok market stall.

temple gate bracelet

Designer: Andrea L. Stern

Finished Size

Approximately 7 inches (17.8 cm) in circumference; adjustable

Materials

10 head pins, each 3 inches (7.6 cm) long

32 Thai silver barrel beads, 4 x 3 mm

20 round Chinese porcelain beads, 6 mm

20 Thai silver puffy rondelle beads, 6 x 4 mm

10 coral glass barrel beads, 10 x 8 mm

15-inch (38.1 cm) length of bracelet wire

56 Czech glass round beads, 4 mm

22 teardrop silver puffy charms, 12 x 9 mm

Tools

Round-nose pliers

Ruler or tape measure

Wire cutters

Heavy-duty wire cutters for bracelet wire (optional)

Crimping pliers

1. To make the connecting bars, take a head pin, and string one small silver barrel, a porcelain bead, one Thai silver rondelle, a coral barrel, a Thai silver rondelle, a porcelain bead, and a small silver barrel.

2. Use the round-nose pliers to make a simple loop at one end of the head pin by bending the wire 90°, approximately ¼ inch (6 mm) from the end, and then turning the loop. Slide the beads down to the loop, and make another simple loop at the other end of the pin.

3. Repeat steps 1 and 2 nine more times, for a total of 10 bars.

4. Use wire cutters to cut the loop of bracelet wire in half. Each piece is approximately 7½ inches (19 cm) in length.

5. Make a tiny loop at one end of the bracelet wire, and string as follows:
   - *Round glass bead
   - Small silver barrel
   Repeat from * two more times, then continue as follows:
   - *Round glass bead
   - Puffy charm
   - Round glass bead
   - Connecting head pin bar
   Repeat from * nine more times, then continue as follows:
   - Round glass bead
   - Puffy charm
   - *Round glass bead
   - Small silver barrel
   Repeat from * two more times, and then end with a round glass bead.

6. Make a tiny loop and close the wire tightly. Crimping pliers are good for this.

7. On the second piece of wire, make a loop and string as follows:
   - *Round glass bead
   - Small silver barrel

   Repeat from * two more times, then continue as follows:
   - Round glass bead
   - Puffy charm
   - Round glass bead

8. Slide wire through the bottom loop of your first connecting bar, and then string another round glass bead, a puffy charm, and another round glass bead.

9. Repeat step 8, sliding the wire through each connecting bar as you go. The wire will want to twist and fight you, but with a little perseverance and some maneuvering, the bracelet will come together.

10. Once all your connecting bars are strung, string a glass bead, then your last puffy charm, and then follow the same bead/barrel pattern you used at the beginning of the wire in step 5. Make another tiny loop with the round-nose pliers, and close the loop with the crimping pliers.

grand tour

This piece includes a potpourri of beads from all over the world. Just imagine it's a record of items you've collected along your journeys.

Designer: Jean Campbell

Finished Size

9¾ inches (24.8 cm) long

Materials

5 grams of root beer seed beads, size 11/0

1 antiqued brass 1-inch (or 24 mm) button with shank

2 gold-filled crimp tubes, 2 x 2 mm

1 white bone wide-holed spacer, 2 x 9 mm

8-inch (20.3 cm) antiqued brass chain, 2 x 4 mm

13 carnelian spacer beads, 4 x 6 mm

1 brown, black, and metallic gold lampworked glass long oval bead, 9 x 25 mm

4 burnt orange dyed bone coin beads with designs, 5 x 16 mm

45 African copper heishi beads, 3.5 mm

2 Bali-style vermeil spacers, 5 x 8 mm

3 gold quartz teardrops with front-to-back hole, 12 x 18 mm

1 brown, black, and metallic gold lampworked glass cube, 12 mm

2 white bone barrels, 6 x 12 mm

8-inch (20.3 cm) length of shiny brass decorative chain, 3 x 4 mm

2 white bone barrels, 6 x 12 mm

10 carnelian melons, 6 mm

10 shiny brass melons, 3 mm

10 gold-filled head pins, 2 inches (5.1 cm) long

Tools

Ruler or tape measure

Wire cutters

Crimping pliers

Bead stop

Chain-nose pliers

Round-nose pliers

1. Cut a 20-inch length (50.8 cm) length of beading wire with the wire cutters. String on approximately 47 seed beads, or enough to fit snugly around the antiqued brass button. (These seed beads will form the loop that holds the toggle of the button to close the bracelet.) Slide the beads to the center of the wire. Gather the wire ends together, and string one crimp tube through both wires. Snug the beads, and use the crimping pliers to crimp the tube.

2. With the wire ends still gathered, string the bone spacer and slide it over the crimp tube.

3. On one end of the wire, string beads as follows:
• Three seed beads
• An end link on the antiqued brass chain
• One carnelian spacer
• Lampworked oval
• One carnelian spacer
• Four seed beads
Then, snug the beads.

5. Again, stretch the antiqued brass chain along the beads just strung, and pass the wire through the closest link. Now string beads in the following order:
- One seed bead
- One carnelian spacer
- Four seed beads
- Lampworked cube
- Four seed beads
- One heishi
- One carnelian spacer followed by one heishi, a total of three times
- Three seed beads

6. Stretch the antiqued brass chain and pass the wire through the closest link. String in the following order:
- Three seed beads
- One coin
- Five seed beads

Pass through the wire through the antiqued brass chain's open end link. Place the bead stop on the wire to hold the beads.

4. Stretch the antiqued brass chain alongside the beads just strung, and pass the wire through the closest link (figure 1). Next, string beads as follows:
- Three seed beads
- One coin
- Seven seed beads
- Three heishi
- One vermeil spacer
- One carnelian spacer
- One teardrop
- One carnelian spacer
- One vermeil spacer
- Three heishi
- Eight seed beads

fig. 1

7. On the other end of the wire, string in the following order:
- Four seed beads
- An end link of the shiny brass chain
- Two seed beads
- Two heishi
- One carnelian spacer
- Two heishi
- Two seed beads
- One coin
- Four seed beads
- Three heishi
- One carnelian spacer
- One teardrop
- One carnelian spacer
- Three heishi
- Three seed beads

8. Stretch the shiny brass chain along the beads just strung and pass the wire through the closest link. Next string in the following order:
- Five seed beads
- One bone barrel
- Five heishi
- One carnelian spacer
- Four heishi
- Three seed beads

9. Stretch the shiny brass chain and pass the wire through the closest link. String in the following order:
- Two seed beads
- One coin
- Three seed beads
- Five heishi
- One carnelian spacer
- Four heishi
- One teardrop
- Three heishi
- Three seed beads

10. Stretch the shiny brass chain and pass through the closest link. String in the following order:
- Two seed beads
- Two heishi
- One bone barrel
- Two heishi
- Three seed beads

11. Stretch the shiny brass chain and pass through the closest link. String six seed beads.

12. Remove the bead stop from the other wire end. Gather the wire ends together and string one crimp tube and the button. Pass both wires back through the crimp tube, snug all the beads, and crimp.

13. Slide one carnelian melon and one brass melon on a head pin. Use the chain-nose and the round-nose pliers to form a wrapped loop that attaches to the fifth link of the brass chain. Repeat the process until you've evenly placed a total of 10 carnelian dangles down the length of brass chain.

How many friends would you like to make a unique little present for? No matter how high the number is, the number of variations you can easily invent for this brooch design is way higher.

savanna brooches

Instructions

Designer: Karen J. Lauseng

Finished Size

1¼ x 1¾ inches (3.2 x 4.4 cm)

Materials

18-gauge nickel silver wire

2 brass spacer beads, 4 mm

African sandstone bead, 8 x 15 mm

2 horn rondelle beads, 6 mm

1 bone bead, 12 x 15 mm

Tools

Pencil and ¼-inch (6 mm) graph paper (several sheets)

String or thread

Ruler or tape measure

Flush cutters

Round-nose pliers

Chain-nose pliers

Jeweler's flat file

Polishing machine or flex shaft (optional)

Fine steel wool

1. Begin by sketching designs on a sheet of ¼-inch (6 mm) graph paper. Your sketch, which will be used as a template for the finished piece, should be the same size as the completed brooch. If you're not inclined to sketch, try making shapes out of copper wire. Inexpensive copper wire, which can be purchased at the hardware store, is easy to shape and fun to experiment with. Make several designs and choose your favorite, or use the one shown in figure 1, which was used to create the brooch at far right in the main photo.

fig. 1

Designer's Tips

You can also use sterling silver wire for this project. However, the advantage of nickel is that, because it's not quite as flexible as silver, it holds up much better.

Feel free to explore the many quick and easy-to-make design possibilities for this brooch. This is a free-form design method, so each piece will be unique. Remember that the key to a successful end product is to place at least one formed loop on the pin portion of the brooch. The loop gives the added spring needed for the pin to stay fastened.

2. To estimate how long the wire should be, run a string along the outline of your design. Measure the string, and add a couple of inches. Using your flush cutters, clip a section of the 18-gauge silver wire to length. A 12-inch (30.5 cm) section is needed for the brooch shown in figure 1. Insert the wire through a brass spacer bead, the African sandstone bead, and a brass spacer bead. Leave one end of the wire about two inches (5.1 cm) longer than the other, and use your hands to bend the wires to the center.

3. Insert both sections of wire through one horn rondelle bead, the bone bead, and the second horn rondelle bead. Using the photo as a guide, bend the wires to the desired shape.

4. To form the pin portion of the brooch, curl the wire using the round-nose pliers to form the loop and provide the spring needed for the catch to remain fastened. Form the curve for the catch with the chain-nose pliers. Use your flush cutter to cut the wires.

5. To finish the piece, use the jeweler's flat file to file the pin to a point and the end of the catch flat. Be sure to remove all cutter marks. Next, polish the point until it is smooth and sharp. If you have a polishing machine, that will work great. If not, rub fine steel wool over the point as you smooth and sharpen it. When the pin is unfastened, the pin stem should point upward and rest about ¼ inch (6 mm) from the top of the catch.

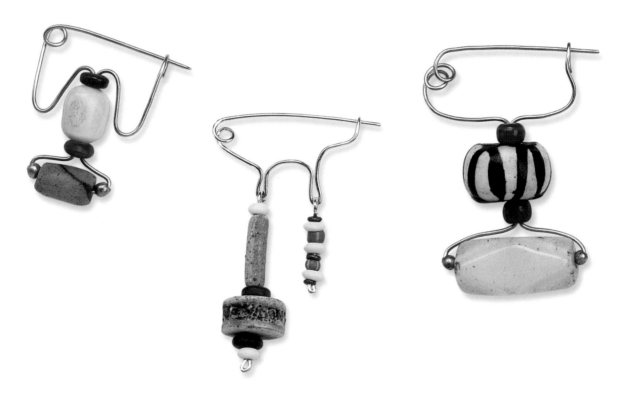

distant oasis

Can't find a camel bell like the one here? Any antique brass bell can add its music to this stunning necklace.

milagros charm
bracelet

Make a bracelet that's jangly
(and just a little bit spooky) with
your choice of milagros ("miracles"),
traditional Latin American healing charms.

Designer: Jean Campbell

Finished Size

9 inches (22.9 cm) long

Materials

18 brass milagros charms, 25 mm

5 shiny brass split rings, 5 x 6 mm

1 gold-filled lobster clasp, 12 mm

Shiny brass decorative chain, 8 inches
(20.3 cm) long, 6 x 8 mm

22 shiny brass head pins, 3 inches (7.6 cm) long

44 shiny black seed beads, size 6/0

18 red, yellow, and black wood barrels,
8 x 12 mm

4 cream/brown wood skull beads, 8 x 12 mm

14 curved brass cylinders, 5 x 6 mm

9 antiqued copper jump rings, 5 x 6 mm

4 vermeil striated cone beads, 4 x 7 mm

2 black onyx ovals, 12 x 20 mm

Antiqued brass jump ring, 7 mm

Red tagua nut slice, 22 x 34 mm

Tools

Metal file

2 chain-nose pliers

Round-nose pliers

Wire cutters

Instructions

1. If necessary, use the metal file to lightly file any sharp edges on the charms. Set aside.

2. Use one split ring to attach the clasp to one end of the chain.

3. To make a barrel bead dangle, take a head pin and slide one seed bead, one wood barrel bead, and a second seed bead onto it. Use the chain-nose and round-nose pliers to form a wrapped loop that attaches the head pin to the same link as the clasp. Skip two links down the chain, and add another barrel bead dangle, taking care to place it on the same side of the link as before. Repeat down the length of the chain to add a total of 18 barrel bead dangles.

4. Take a head pin and slide one seed bead, one skull bead, one brass cylinder, and a second seed bead onto it. Form a wrapped loop that attaches to the sixth chain link. Repeat for the 16th, 24th, and 32nd links, adding a total of four skull dangles.

5. Use chain-nose pliers to open one copper jump ring. Slip the ring through a milagros charm and the first chain link, positioning the charm so it's opposite the wood dangle (figure 1). Close the ring. Repeat down the chain to add all the charms.

   fig. 1

6. Take a head pin and slide one cone, one oval, and one cone onto it. Form a wrapped loop to secure the beads, and set aside. Repeat to make a second onyx dangle.

7. Use a split ring to connect both onyx dangles to the chain's open-end link.

8. Connect the brass jump ring to the tagua slice. Use a copper jump ring to connect this charm to the second link from the chain's end, next to the onyx dangles.

moroccan buds

Find a pair of vintage enameled beads you'd love to show off, and you're halfway home to wearing these easy-to-make earrings.

Instructions

Designer: Terry Taylor

Finished Size

Each: 2¾ inches (7 cm) long

Materials

2 sterling silver eye pins

2 vintage silver Moroccan drops

4 gemstone beads

2 enameled Moroccan beads

2 sterling silver ear wires

Tools

Round-nose pliers

Wire cutters

Designer's Tip

To create a natural, unified look, make sure the enameled beads and the drops include silver with a similarly antique appearance.

1. Thread the silver drops onto the eye pins.

2. Top each drop with a gemstone bead of your choice.

3. Thread the enameled beads onto the pins, and top each with a gemstone bead.

4. Use the round-nose pliers to attach the beads to each ear wire with a wrapped loop. Trim any excess with wire cutters.

silk road

Use pliers and a jewelry-making jig to plot the twists and turns of the brass wires that link this collection of Chinese porcelain beads.

Instructions

1. This project requires that you make two different patterns out of the brass wire, so you'll need to set up a jig. You can either make your own (see tip box), or use a purchased jewelry-making jig.

2. Use the chain-nose pliers to create a loop at one end of your wire. Place the loop on the jig peg, and then wrap the wire around the jig pegs to create the link. (Figure 1 shows a half-completed link.) Remove the link from the jig, use the wire cutters to trim the wire, and file smooth with cup burr or needle file. Straighten wires as necessary. Harden links with the hammer and anvil or steel block. Repeat until you've created five links in this same shape.

fig. 1

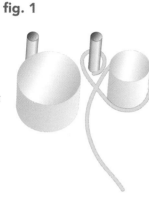

3. Set up the jig for the second link shape and repeat the same process as in step 2 until you've made four links in this second shape.

Designer's Tips

Although it's easy to make your own jig, you can also purchase a jewelry-making jig. The advantage of a manufactured jig is that it's reusable. It also has a clear base, so it's easy to draw a design on a piece of paper and then place the jig over the design to determine where to insert the pegs.

But if you want to make a homemade jig, here's how. Assemble a block of wood, five nails, and three tubular beads or objects (cut pipe works well). Hammer the nails into the block. Slide the beads onto the nails.

Designers: Elizabeth Glass Geltman and Rachel Geltman

Finished Size

28 inches (71.1 cm) long

Materials

16-gauge brass round wire

19 Chinese porcelain beads in varied sizes, shapes, and colors

Block of wood (optional)

Five nails (optional)

Three tubular beads or objects (optional; cut pipe works well here)

Tools

Chain-nose pliers

Jewelry-making jig

Wire cutters

Cup burr or needle file

Rawhide, plastic, or chasing hammer

Steel bench block or anvil

Ruler or tape measure

Round-nose pliers

Permanent marker (optional)

4. Set the links aside, and assemble the beaded links. Cut about 2 to 3 inches (5.1 to 7.6 cm) of wire, depending on bead size. Slide the bead onto the wire. Use the round-nose pliers to make a loop on either side of the bead. Trim the wire, and file until smooth to the touch. Adjust loops with pliers so they are snug against the bead and the loops are nicely rounded. Repeat until you have created 19 beaded links.

5. Assemble the necklace. Using your chain-nose pliers to open the loops, connect your links and beaded loops together to create a chain.

6. To make the clasp, cut 3 inches (7.6 cm) of wire and use the round-nose pliers to make a small loop at one end. Pull the looped end of the wire around your forefinger. Next, while holding the looped end, pull the wire around the forefinger of your other hand. Trim the wire and file until smooth. Pull one end into a scroll shape. Harden with the hammer and anvil or steel block.

7. Attach the clasp.

Designer's Tip

To create uniform-sized loops, mark your pliers with a permanent marker and create the loops on this line.

ocean reflection

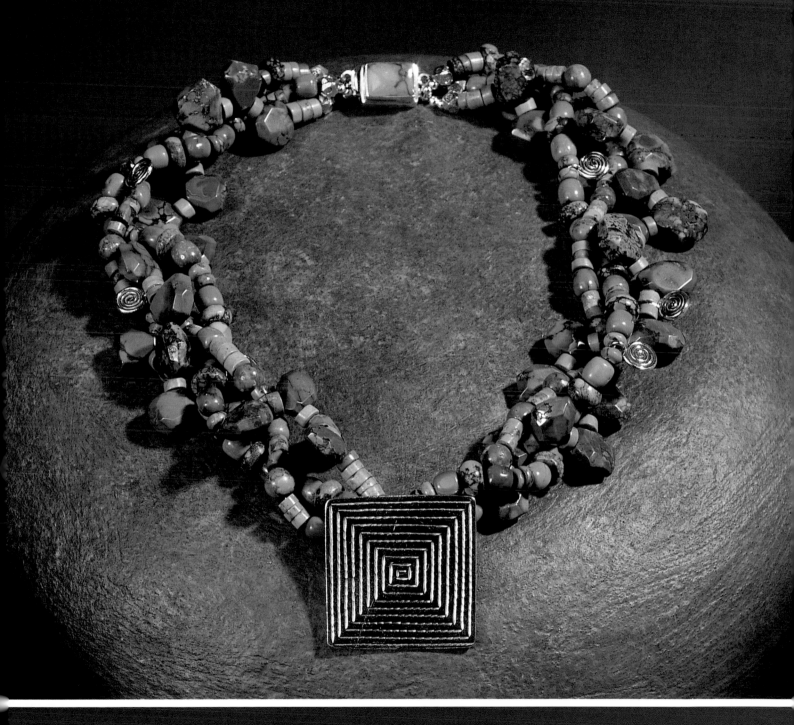

Silver from Thailand rides a blue-green cascade
of faceted stones and variously shaped beads.

ocean reflection

Designer: Sherry Duquet

Finished Size

18 inches (45.7 cm) long

Materials

3 lengths of 0.014-inch (0.4 mm) beading wire, each 24 inches (61 cm)

148 turquoise flat-sided rondelles, ranging from 3 to 4 mm

48 turquoise rounded rectangles, ranging from 7 to 8 mm

12 turquoise rounds, 8 mm

Hill Tribes silver square pendant, 38 mm

20 turquoise large rounded-edge rondelles, 3 to 5 mm

32 turquoise small rounded-edge rondelles, 1 to 3 mm

6 Hill Tribes silver drops, 9 x 13 mm

36 turquoise top-drilled faceted teardrops, 13 x 17 mm

6 Hill Tribes silver octagon beads, 6 mm

6 sterling silver round finishing beads, 3 mm

6 sterling silver crimp tubes, 2 x 2 mm

Tape (optional)

Sterling silver and turquoise 2-strand box clasp

6 sterling silver crimp covers, 3 mm

Tools

Ruler or tape measure

Bevel cutters

Beading board

Crimping pliers

Flat-nose pliers

1. Measure and cut three 24-inch (61 cm) lengths of beading wire with the bevel cutters.

2. Begin the first strand on the bead board by sliding the beads onto a 24-inch (61 cm) length of beading wire in the following order:
   • 3 flat-sided rondelles
   • Rounded rectangle
   • 3 flat-sided rondelles
   • 8-mm round bead
   Repeat this pattern until you've used seven rounded rectangles and six 8-mm rounds.

3. Once you've placed the seventh rounded rectangle, use four flat-sided rondelles instead of three, and place the Hill Tribes silver square pendant on the wire.

4. Immediately on the other side of the pendant, slide four flat-sided rondelles, one rounded rectangle, three flat-sided rondelles, and an 8-mm round bead. From this point, repeat the step 2 pattern five times. Next, string three flat-sided rondelles, a rounded rectangle, and three flat-sided rondelles. Finish the strand by placing a rounded rectangles on each end of the wire.

5. Begin the second strand on the bead board by sliding three flat-sided rondelles onto the second 24-inch (61 cm) length of beading wire.

6. Add beads in the following order:
   • Large rounded-edge rondelle
   • Flat-sided rondelle
   • Large rounded-edge rondelle
   • Flat-sided rondelle

7. Next, slide beads onto the strand in the following order:
   • Rounded rectangle
   • Large rounded-edge rondelle
   • Rounded rectangle
   • 2 small rounded-edge rondelles

8. Repeat the pattern in step 7 one time, but insert a Hill Tribes silver drop between the last two small rondelles. Repeat the pattern in step 7 three more times, inserting a silver drop between the last two small rondelles on the third repetition. Repeat the pattern three more times, and slide the strand through the Hill Tribes silver square pendant.

9. Immediately on the other side of the pendant, place two small rounded-edge rondelles. Repeat the pattern in step 7 six times, inserting a silver drop between the last two small rondelles on every third repetition. Repeat the pattern in step 7 once.

10. Finish the second strand by stringing beads in the following order:
- Rounded rectangle
- Large rondelle
- Rounded rectangle
- Flat-sided rondelle
- Large rondelle
- Flat-sided rondelle
- Large rondelle
- 3 flat-sided rondelles

11. Begin the third strand on the bead board by sliding three flat-sided rondelles onto a 24-inch (61 cm) length of beading wire. Then alternate one turquoise teardrop with one flat-sided rondelle ten times. Place a Hill Tribes silver drop, followed by a flat-sided rondelle.

12. Next, alternate one turquoise teardrop with one flat-sided rondelle nine times. Add five flat-sided rondelles, and then string the strand through the pendant.

13. Place six flat-sided rondelles immediately on the other side of the pendant. Alternate one teardrop with one flat-sided rondelle nine times. Place a Hill Tribes silver drop, followed by a flat-sided rondelle.

14. Then alternate one turquoise teardrop with one flat-sided rondelle 10 times. Finish the strand with two flat-sided rondelles.

15. To finish the necklace, begin by placing a Hill Tribes silver octagon bead, a 3-mm sterling silver round finishing bead, and a sterling silver crimp tube on the ends of each strand.

16. Lay out necklace with all three strands separated to prepare for braiding. Braid three strands on one side of the pendant.

Designer's Tip

In step 16, tape down the opposite side of the three strands to the table to hold them firmly in place while braiding.

17. Take one end of the clasp and thread beading wire from one strand at a time through one of the holes. Feed beading wire back through the crimp tube, 3-mm bead, Hill Tribes silver octagon, and several of the gemstone beads, if possible. Pull the wire snugly, but not too tightly, and crimp one strand at a time, trimming excess wire. Use the crimping pliers to crimp the crimp tube firmly around the wire, one strand at a time.

18. Repeat steps 16 and 17 on the other side of the pendant.

19. Using the flat-nose pliers, close crimp covers around the crimp tubes of each strand on both sides.

cameroon lariat

Elemental and elegant, this piece has two unconnected ends. Follow the directions at the end of the project for wearing it, or blaze your own path.

Instructions

1. With the beading wire still attached to the spool, string a crimp bead, followed by 4 inches (10.2 cm) of seed beads. Next, string three brass beads; the brass beads should slide over the seed beads.

2. String the wire end back through the crimp bead. Close the crimp with the crimping pliers, taking care to keep the wires from crossing inside the crimp beads. Use the wire cutters to trim the wire tail close to the crimp.

3. Measure 48 inches (1.2 m) of beading wire past the crimp bead. Cut the wire at this point. String one brass bead, followed by 41½ inches (1.1 m) of seed beads. The brass bead will cover your crimp from step 2.

4. String a crimp bead, then 4 inches (10.2 cm) of seed beads.

5. String four brass beads. Push one brass bead past the crimp and leave the other three beads on the other side of the crimp (figure 1).

fig. 1

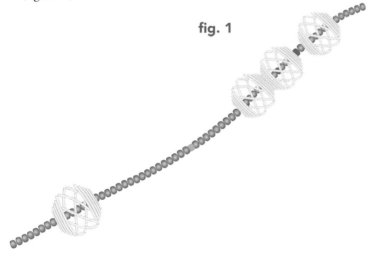

6. Repeat step 2, after making sure before you crimp that the last three beads are on the loop you've formed.

7. Cover both crimps with the brass beads that are not on the loops. To wear the lariat, fold the strand in half. Place the lariat around your neck and tuck the looped ends through the fold as though you are wearing a scarf. Pull the loops until the lariat is a comfortable length.

Designer: Catherine Hodge

Finished Size

45½ inches (1.2 m) long

Materials

54 inches (1.4 m) of 0.019-inch (0.5 mm) beading wire

2 crimp beads, 2 x 2 mm

Matte fuchsia seed beads, size 10/0

8 West African brass beads, ranging from 10 to 12 mm, each with 3-mm holes (measurements for handmade beads are approximate)

Tools

Ruler or tape measure

Crimping pliers

Wire cutters

This showstopping piece
marries sight with sound.
The antique bell from India
is surrounded by beads of
turquoise and sponge coral.

mumbai melody

Instructions

Designer: Jamie Cloud Eakin

Finished Size

21 inches (53.3 cm) long

Materials

63 20-gauge jump rings, 5 mm

42 metal bells, 6 mm

22 inches (55.9 cm) flexible beading wire

2 crimp beads

Hook-and-eye clasp

34 round gold beads, 4 mm

20 irregular sponge coral beads, 8 x 10 mm

16 gold flower spacer beads, 4 mm

Turquoise heishi beads, 6 x 3 mm

Metal bell from India, or other pendant as desired

Tools

2 needle-nose pliers

6 small safety pins

Ruler or tape measure

Wire cutters

Crimping pliers

1. To make the bell jangles, use both needle-nose pliers to open a jump ring and put on one small bell. Close the jump ring. Repeat five more times so you have a total of six bell/jump ring sets.

2. Open a jump ring, and put one end through four of the bell/jump ring sets from step 1. Close the jump ring.

3. Open a jump ring, and put on one small bell. Put the jump ring with bell through the two center jump rings of the four from step 2. Close the jump ring (figure 1).

fig. 1

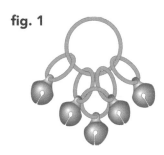

4. Open a jump ring. String in the following order:
   • One safety pin
   • One jump ring with bell attached from step 1
   • Jump ring from steps 2 and 3 above
   • One jump ring with bell attached from step 1
   The safety pin will be removed later, so be sure to go through the section of the pin that opens. This is simply a tool to help keep track of which jump ring to go though when making the necklace (figure 2).

fig. 2

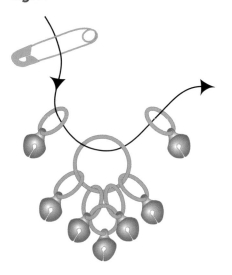

5. Repeat steps 1 through 4 five more times for a total of six bell sections.

6. To make the necklace, use the wire cutters to cut 22 inches (55.9 cm) of flexible beading wire. Put on one crimp bead near one end. String the wire through the loop on the hook end of the clasp and then back through the crimp bead. Use the crimping pliers to crimp the bead, and trim so the short tail is long enough to fit underneath a 4-mm bead.

String the necklace beads in the following order. (After you've used the safety pin on the bell sections to help you identify which jump ring to pass through, you can remove the safety pin.)
• Gold bead, coral bead, gold bead, coral bead, gold bead
• Spacer, three turquoise heishi, spacer
• Gold bead, coral bead, gold bead, coral bead, gold bead
• Spacer, three turquoise heishi, spacer
• Gold bead, coral bead, gold bead
• Jump ring with bells
• Gold bead, coral bead, gold bead
• Spacer, three turquoise heishi, spacer
• Gold bead, coral bead, gold bead
• Jump ring with bells
• Gold bead, coral bead, gold bead
• Spacer, three turquoise heishi, spacer
• Gold bead, coral bead, gold bead
• Jump ring with bells
• Gold bead, coral bead

7. String on the large bell pendant.

8. On the other side of the bell pendant, repeat step 7 in reverse order.

9. Pick up one crimp bead and the eye part of the clasp. String back through the crimp bead and the 4-mm bead.

10. Pull to adjust the tension and then crimp the crimp bead. Trim the end.

afternoon bazaar

In this colorful set, stunning medleys of African beads are separated by multifaceted silver spacers from Thailand.

Instructions

Designer: Sherry Duquet

Finished Size

Necklace: 21½ inches (54.6 cm) long
Bracelet: 8 inches (20.3 cm) long

Materials

33 inches (83.8 cm) of 0.014-inch
(0.4 mm) flexible beading wire

44 mixed African trade beads, ranging from
8 to 25 mm

23 Hill Tribes small silver spacer beads, 3 mm

2 Hill Tribes silver spacer beads, 7 mm

4 sterling silver round finishing beads, 3 mm

4 sterling silver crimp tubes, 2 x 2 mm

Sterling silver hook extender clasp

4 sterling silver crimp covers, 3 mm

7 sterling silver rondelles, 4 mm

Sterling silver toggle clasp, 15-mm circle, 24-mm bar

Tools

Bevel cutters

Beading board

Ruler or tape measure

Crimping pliers

Flat-nose pliers

Nonsticky silicone plastic putty
(optional)

1. To make the necklace, begin by using the bevel cutters to cut a 23-inch (58.4 cm) length of beading wire. On the beading board, plan the arrangement of 31 African trade beads, interspersed with 3-mm and 7-mm Hill Tribes silver spacer beads as needed. String the beads in a graduated fashion, with the largest beads in the center. Finish stringing by placing a 3-mm Hill Tribes silver spacer bead, a 3-mm silver round finishing bead, and a crimp tube on each end.

2. Take one end of the extender clasp and thread beading wire through the hole. Feed the beading wire back through the crimp tube, 3-mm bead, Hill Tribes silver bead, and if possible, one African bead, hiding the wire end in the bead. Using the crimping pliers, crimp the crimping tube firmly around the wire.

3. Take the other end of the extender clasp, pull the wire through snugly, and repeat step 2.

4. Before crimping the second end, pull the wire snugly, but not too tightly. Crimp and trim any excess wire. Use the flat-nose pliers to close the 3-mm crimp covers around the crimp tubes on both sides.

5. To make the bracelet, begin by using the bevel cutters to cut a 10-inch (25.4 cm) length of beading wire. On the beading board, plan out a design using 13 mixed African trade beads interspersed with five sterling silver rondelles. String the beads, one at a time, onto the beading wire. Finish by placing one sterling silver rondelle, a 3-mm silver finishing bead, and a crimp tube on each end. You can place the putty on one end to hold beads in place.

6. Take one end of the toggle clasp and thread beading wire through the hole. Feed beading wire back through the crimp tube, 3-mm finishing bead, silver rondelle, and one African bead, hiding the wire end in the bead. Use the crimping pliers to crimp the crimping tube firmly around wire. Remove the putty from the opposite end.

7. Take the other end of the toggle clasp, pull the wire through snugly, and repeat step 6.

8. Before crimping the second end, pull the wire firmly, but not too tightly, then crimp and trim any excess wire. Use the flat-nose pliers to close 3-mm crimp covers around the crimp tubes on both sides.

Designer's Tip

Silicone plastic putty is a great tool to keep the beads on one end from sliding off while crimping the opposite end. It doesn't stick to the wire or the beads.

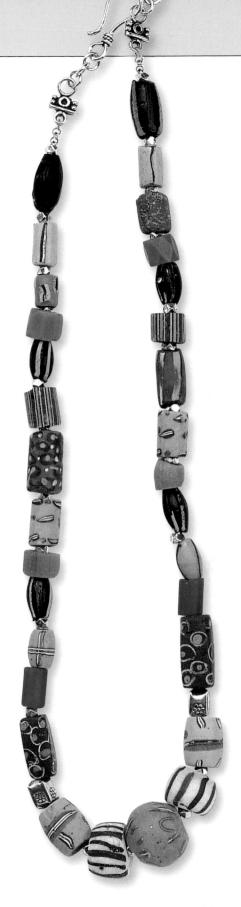

The ancient Chinese text of the *I Ching* describes a system for uncovering the order in chance events. In beading this project, you can follow the photo closely, or just see where chance takes you.

i ching coin earrings

Instructions

Designer: Terry Taylor

Finished Size

Each: 2¼ inches (5.7 cm) long

Materials

2 replica Chinese *I Ching* coins

4 brass or gold-filled head pins

4 small brass beads

8 small brass washer beads

8 African bronze beads

Dyed coral slices

2 bronze ear wires

Tools

Sharp nail or automatic center punch

Drill and small drill bit
(#60 or smaller)

Chain-nose pliers

Round-nose pliers

Wire cutters

Designer's Tip

Make the hanging lengths of beads as long as you wish. If you want to hang a third length on a coin, you'll need to choose smaller beads.

1. Use the nail or center punch to make two evenly spaced marks along the lower edge of each coin. Use the drill and small drill bit to make small holes in the coins.

2. Thread the brass beads, brass washers, bronze beads, and coral slices onto the head pins. Thread the beads symmetrically, if you wish, or create subtle visual interest by varying the position of the small brass beads and washer beads.

3. Use the chain-nose and round-nose pliers to bend the straight end of a beaded head pin into the beginning loop for a wrapped loop. Thread the head pin onto a coin, and finish the wrapped loop. Trim any excess wire with wire cutters.

4. Repeat step 3 for each of the other three head pins.

5. Use chain-nose pliers to open one ear wire, attach the coin to the top hole, and then close. Repeat for the second coin.

zambezi journey

Some pieces just seem to come from a distant place and time. Few who see you wear this African-inspired necklace will even imagine it was made in this country and this century.

Instructions

Designer: Andrea L. Stern

Finished Size

19 inches (48.3 cm) long

Materials

Nylon beading thread, size FFF or comparable

African brass pendant

34 striped beads, size 6/0

3 coral glass tube beads, 15 x 7 mm

African brass bead

16- to 18-inch (40.6 to 45.7 cm) strand of sand-cast rondelle beads, 5 mm

4 cast-brass tube beads, 12 mm

2 bead tips

Toggle clasp

Tools

Ruler or tape measure

Scissors

Tweezers

Bead-tip cement or nail polish

Flat-nose pliers

1. Use the scissors to cut a 24-inch (61 cm) length of your beading thread, and pull it tightly to stretch it out. (If you skip this step, the weight of the pendant will eventually cause your necklace to stretch.)

2. Thread the pendant onto the thread, centering it so you now have two threads to bead on. String through both threads one striped bead, one coral glass tube, a striped bead, and then the African brass bead.

3. String beads on each individual thread as follows:
   • 5 sand-cast rondelle beads
   • Striped bead
   • Cast-brass tube bead
   • Striped bead
   • 5 sand-cast rondelle beads
   • Striped bead
   • Coral glass tube bead
   • Striped bead
   • 5 sand-cast rondelle beads
   • Striped bead
   • Cast-brass tube bead

4. For the rest of the necklace, repeat the following pattern 10 times:
   • 5 sand-cast beads
   • Striped bead

5. End with as many sand-cast rondelle beads as needed to make both strands of equal length.

6. String thread through the hole in the bead tip. Using tweezers, make a knot and pull tightly to gather the knot as closely to the bead tip as possible. (Make a loop in the thread, place tweezers inside the loop, and grab the base thread at the base of the bead tip; pull the thread down to the knot; repeat.) Glue the knot with bead-tip cement or nail polish. Let dry, and then trim. Using the flat-nose pliers, close the bead tip.

7. Put the loop of the bead tip through the loop on the clasp and close the loop. Repeat.

turtle story

A Native American tradition holds that the world was formed on the back of a turtle. You'll have to make up your own story to explain where the second turtle on this focal bead came from.

Instructions

Designers: Elizabeth Glass Geltman and Rachel Geltman

Finished Size

27 inches (68.6 cm) long

Materials

16-gauge sterling silver round wire

Beading wire

8 sterling silver crimp beads

48 sterling silver Bali daisy spacer beads

4 strands hessonite garnets, each 16 inches (40.6 cm) long

2 sterling silver bead cones

Petrified wood beads, ranging from 6 to 10 mm

6 sterling silver Bali bead caps in two different styles

Carved bone turtle bead

S clasp

Tools

Ruler or tape measure

Wire cutters

Chain-nose pliers

Round-nose pliers

Crimping pliers

Cup burr or needle file

Mandrel or small marker (optional)

Steel bench block or anvil (optional)

Rawhide, plastic, or chasing hammer (optional)

1. Use the wire cutters to cut two 3-inch (7.6 cm) lengths of 16-gauge sterling silver round wire.

2. With the chain-nose and round-nose pliers, create a wrapped loop at one end of the first wire. Repeat with the second wire. Set the second wire aside.

3. Cut 20 inches (50.8 cm) of beading wire. Feed the beading wire through the loop at the end of one of the pieces of prepared silver round wire, add a crimp bead to the beading wire, and crimp with the crimping pliers.

4. Next, slide two sterling silver Bali daisy spacer beads onto the beading wire. Then string one 16-inch (40.6 cm) strand of hessonite garnets and Bali spacer beads in the desired pattern. Crimp the other end of the beading wire onto the loop of the second piece of round silver wire.

5. Repeat steps 3 and 4 until all four bead strands are strung with hessonite garnets and Bali spacer beads and attached to the loops at the end of both pieces of the round silver wire.

6. Pick up the piece of round silver wire and feed it through the bead cone; wrap the silver wire end to secure. Trim as needed. File the ends with the cup burr or needle file until smooth. The bead cone should hide the four crimped ends.

7. Repeat at the other end of the strung necklace.

8. Cut 3 inches (7.6 cm) of silver round wire. Feed the silver wire through the end loop of your project necklace and create a wrapped loop. Slide a 10-mm petrified wood bead onto the silver round wire, and wrap to secure. This step will begin the process of attaching the wire-wrapped portion to the strung portion of the necklace.

9. Cut 5 inches (12.7 cm) of silver round wire, feed the silver wire through the end loop of your project necklace, and create a wrapped loop. Slide a Bali bead cap, a 10-mm petrified wood bead, and a matching Bali bead cap onto the silver wire. Slide the bone turtle bead onto the open end of the silver round wire and create a large wire wrap to secure. Trim as necessary and file smooth.

10. Cut another 5 inches (12.7 cm) of the sterling silver round wire, feed the wire through the second hole in the bone turtle bead, and create a large wire wrap to secure. Slide a Bali bead cap, a 10-mm petrified wood bead, and a matching Bali bead cap onto the wire, and wrap to secure.

11. Cut 3 more inches (7.6 cm) of silver round wire. Feed the wire through the end loop of your project necklace, and create a wrapped loop. Slide a 10-mm petrified wood bead onto the wire, and wrap to secure.

12. Repeat step 11, this time sliding a different-style Bali bead cap, a 10-mm petrified wood bead, and a matching Bali bead cap onto the wire, and wrap to secure.

13. At the opposite end of the necklace, repeat step 8.

14. Attach the clasp to the necklace.

Designer's Tips

This necklace is strung to be asymmetrical. You can wear it with the turtle bead centered if you wish, or put the turtle to one side for a different look.

You can create your own S clasps. First, cut 2 inches (5.1 cm) of 16-gauge sterling silver round wire. File both ends of the wire until it's smooth, using a needle file or cup burr. Wrap one end of the wire around the end of a mandrel. (A small marker or thick pencil works well as a mandrel.) Then wrap the other end of the wire around the mandrel in the opposite direction. Harden the wire by hitting it on an anvil with a hammer or mallet. Finally, adjust the clasp with your pliers as necessary until it's the desired size and shape.

A stunning amber centerpiece like this needs a strong setting, and twined strands of amber, peridot, red coral, and lapis lazuli do the job beautifully.

Instructions

Designer: Sherry Duquet

Finished Size

19½ inches (49.5 cm) long

Materials

Large amber nugget

4 pieces of silver 24-gauge dead soft wire, each 8½ inches (21.6 cm) long

4 25-inch (63.5 cm) lengths of 0.014-inch (0.4 mm) flexible beading wire

200 lapis rondelles, ranging from 1 to 3 mm

18 assorted sterling silver spacer beads, ranging from 2 to 4 mm

250 faceted peridot rondelles, ranging from 1 to 2 mm

150 amber chips, ranging from 4 to 6 mm

140 red coral rondelles, ranging from 2.5 to 3 mm

6 red coral beads, ranging from 5 to 7 mm

8 sterling silver tube-shaped spacer beads, 5 mm

8 sterling silver round finishing beads, 3 mm

8 sterling silver crimp tubes, 2 x 2 mm

Sterling silver and red coral four-strand box clasp

8 sterling silver crimp covers, 3 mm

Tools

Protective eyewear and gloves

Small motorized cutting tool with a ¹⁄₁₆ drill bit and a 482 collet

Ruler or tape measure

Sturdy wire cutters

Object with 15 mm diameter for wrapping (tool handle, round tube, etc.)

Crimping pliers

1. Using the cutting tool's highest speed position, drill two evenly spaced holes through the amber in short, quick motions so that the nugget hangs level. Withdraw the bit every few seconds so that the bit doesn't break. Amber does get hot, and sometimes small melting pieces will fly off, so make sure you wear protective glasses and gloves.

2. Next, use two pieces of the 24-gauge wire to thread and twist through each drilled hole in the amber, and then create the 15-mm wrapped loops. (Once completed, the pendant will slide over the necklace strands.) First, measure and use the wire cutters to cut the silver wire. Then wrap the wire around a round object with a 15-mm diameter (for example, a tool handle). Twist the wire tail around the stem of the loop several times to secure firmly (figure 1). Set aside the pendant.

fig. 1

3. Using the beading board to arrange your beads, begin to slide lapis rondelles, one at a time, onto one of the 25-inch (63.5 cm) lengths of beading wire. Randomly intersperse eight or nine of the assorted silver spacer beads. Repeat to create peridot and amber chip strands.

4. Slide red coral rondelles onto a 25-inch (63.5 cm) length of beading wire one at a time. Randomly intersperse the six larger red coral beads and eight or nine of the assorted silver spacer beads.

Beading board

Bevel cutters

Flat-nose pliers

5. Place a silver spacer tube, a 3-mm silver round finishing bead, and a crimp tube on the ends of each of the above strands.

6. Take one end of the box clasp and thread the beading wire from one strand through one of the holes. Repeat with the other three strands.

7. For each strand, feed the strand of wire back through the crimp tube, 3-mm bead, silver spacer tube, and several of the gemstone beads. Pull the wire snugly, but not too tightly, and crimp the crimp tube firmly around the wire, one strand at a time. Use the bevel cutters to trim the excess wire.

8. Twist the four strands as shown in the photo. Line up the strands so that after each strand loops loosely around the other strands, its beading wire ends up in the same corresponding hole on each side of the clasp. (For example, the lapis strand will end up in the first clasp loop on both sides of the clasp.) Then repeat steps 6 and 7 on the other side of the box clasp until all four strands are crimped.

9. Use the crimping pliers to close the crimp covers around the crimp tubes on the ends of each strand.

10. Gently slide the amber pendant over the tab insert side of the clasp until it's positioned in the center of the necklace.

Designer's Tip

The crimping pliers are a handy finishing tool to smooth the cut end of the wire once you are done twisting in step 2.

bones of old

A curved bone focal bead combines with beads in shades of bone and brown to make a necklace with a look directly from the plains of Africa.

Instructions

1. Use the diagonal or flush cutters to cut a piece of beading wire that's long enough to go over your head and will accommodate your design. Allow 4 extra inches (10.2 cm) to work with on each end.

2. Lay out the beads in a series of repeated patterns. Begin by putting the focal bead in the center of your wire. Place a disc bead and a round bead on each side.

3. Continue with the following two patterns on each side:
   • Crosscut bone bead, round bead, crosscut bone bead
   • Round bead, disc bead, round bead
   Repeat this two-pattern sequence three times.

4. Thread the ending pattern on both sides of the wire: crosscut bone bead, round bead, crosscut bone bead. Continue with this bead pattern to the end of your wire length.

5. Holding on to each end, fit the beaded wire around your neck to see if it's long enough and if you like the composition. Adjust the bead sets accordingly.

6. Remove the last two beads on one end of the wire, add a crimp, and replace the beads. Repeat on the other end of the wire.

7. Holding the wire ends in each hand, make sure that all the beads are draping snugly. Then slide the wire from one end of the necklace through the end beads, the crimp bead, and the next two beads. Repeat the process with the other end.

8. Using the crimping pliers, crimp first one side. After making sure that the beads have not loosened on the wire, crimp the other side. Do this step carefully, as the crimps can easily slip into the beads on either side.

Designer: Marilyn Peters

Finished Size

28 inches (71.1 cm) long

Materials

0.019-inch (.5 mm) beading wire

African comma-shaped bone focal bead

8 disc beads with brown accents

31 round beads with cream accents

24 long oval crosscut bone-colored beads

2 gold-colored crimp beads

Tools

Ruler or tape measure

Diagonal or flush cutters

Crimping pliers

The most crucial step in this project comes at the start: finding a silver pendant and two large beads with just the right detail and patina to give this necklace the look of a treasured antique.

silver dragon

Instructions

Designer: Andrea L. Stern

Finished Size

21 inches (53.3 cm) long

Materials

3 turquoise cones, 25 x 9 mm

3 silver head pins, each 3 inches (7.6 cm) long

Chinese silver dragon pendant with two loops on top and three loops on bottom, 60 x 65 mm

4 12-inch (30.5 cm) pieces of 0.019-inch (0.5 mm) flexible beading wire

6 crimp beads

16 Chinese turquoise beads, 4 mm

16 Chinese turquoise beads, ranging from 6 to 7 mm

26 silver flower filler beads, 6 mm

28 Chinese turquoise beads, ranging from 9 to 10 mm

2 Chinese silver dragon tubes, 50 x 15 mm

Hook-and-eye clasp

Tools

Chain-nose pliers

Ruler or tape measure

Wire cutters

Round-nose pliers

Scissors

Crimping pliers

1. Use the turquoise cones to make three dangles by stringing each one onto a head pin. Use the chain-nose pliers to bend the wire 90°at the top, and then use the wire cutters to trim ⅝ inch (1.6 cm) from the end. After using the round-nose pliers to make a big loop, string each cone onto the bottom of the pendant and close the loop.

2. Measure and cut a 12-inch (30.5 cm) piece of the beading wire with the scissors. Slide the wire through a crimp bead, through the loop on one side of the dragon pendant, and then back through the crimp bead. Crimp with the crimping pliers. Trim the excess wire close to the bead. Repeat, sliding the second piece of wire through the same loop on the top of the pendant.

3. String beads onto each wire in the following order:
   • 4-mm Chinese turquoise bead
   • 6- to 7-mm Chinese turquoise bead
   • Silver flower bead
   • 9- to 10-mm Chinese turquoise bead
   • Silver flower bead
   • 6- to 7-mm Chinese turquoise bead
   • 4-mm Chinese turquoise bead

4. Slide both wires through the long silver dragon tube. (Hint: it's easier to slide one wire at a time.) Separate wires and then repeat step 3.

5. After stringing both wires through a silver flower bead, string them through a 9- to 10-mm Chinese turquoise bead and a flower bead a total of four times.

6. String six more 9- to 10-mm Chinese turquoise beads onto both wires.

7. Pass both wires through a crimp bead, through one side of the clasp, and then back through the crimp bead and crimp. Trim close to the bead.

8. Repeat steps 2 through 7 on the other side of the pendant.

endless circle

To make the barrel-shaped beads
used here, the Krobo tribe of
Ghana powders old broken glass,
layers different colors of powder
in a mold—similar to making a
sand sculpture in a bottle—and
then melts it into something new.

Instructions

Designer: Mike Ann Zable

Finished Size

24½ inches (62.2 cm) long

Materials

Small kasmiri bead to fit in the opening in the focal bead

1 or 2 round agate beads, 2 mm (optional)

2½-inch (6.4 cm) sterling silver head pin with decorative head

Open oval focal bead with vertical hole in the top, 1½ x 1⅛ inches (3.8 x 2.9 cm) long

32-inch (81.3 cm) length of 0.019-inch (0.5 mm) flexible beading wire

8 aventurine rondelles, 4 mm

2 long oval horn eye beads, 25 mm

10 Christmas trade beads, 4 mm

10 hand-painted Kazuri pit-a-pat beads, approximately 20 mm

10 bird-shaped beads, approximately 10 mm

18 small Krobo beads, 5 to 10 mm

2 Kazuri ting-ting beads, 15 mm

Horn toggle clasp

4 silver crimp beads, 2 mm

Tools

Round-nose pliers

Wire cutters

Ruler or measuring tape

Beading board

Crimping pliers

1. First, make the focal pendant. Thread the kasmiri bead and, if desired, one or two very small agate beads on the head pin. Run the top of the head pin up through the hole in the focal bead pendant. Using the round-nose pliers, make a wrapped loop from the end of the head pin.

2. Using the wire cutters, cut a 32-inch (81.3 cm) length of flexible beading wire. Use a beading board to lay out the beads, starting with the focal pendent on the number zero. Place beads in a uniform pattern up both sides from the center, ending the pattern when you reach the desired length. There should be an extra 3½ inches (8.9 cm) of wire on each side.

3. Attach one piece of the toggle clasp to each side and use the crimping pliers to fasten securely with one or two crimp beads on each side.

Designer's Tip

A necklace 24 inches (61 cm) or larger can fit over an average person's head without undoing the clasp.

copper jangle

Wire-looped charms hang from a chain; bone beads hang from the
ends of the charms; and the whole design hangs together beautifully.

Designer: Cindy Kinerson

Finished Size

7¾ inches (19.7 cm) long

Materials

5 feet (1.5 m) of 20-gauge copper wire

7-inch (17.8 cm) length of copper link chain

21 assorted bone beads

6 red horn spacer beads

5 gold horn spacer beads

6 copper beads

4 red-colored white heart beads

Copper toggle clasp

Tools

Wire cutters

Ruler or tape measure

Round-nose pliers

2 chain-nose pliers

Instructions

1. Use the wire cutters to cut the copper wire in 3-inch (7.6 cm) lengths. You'll need as many pieces of wire as you have links in your chain.

2. To make the charms: Thread the first inch (2.5 cm) of one 3-inch (7.6 cm) length of wire through a bone bead. Bend the 1-inch section of the wire at a 90° angle, and wrap it twice around the other approximately 2-inch (5.1 cm) section of the wire. Place one of the spacer, copper, or white heart beads above the wrapped wire, and then use your round-nose pliers to form a loop with the straight end of the wire (figure 1). Make two wraps below the loop, and trim off the excess with the wire cutters. Use your chain-nose pliers to help adjust the wire wraps so they're tight. Repeat with all of the bone beads.

fig. 1

3. To assemble the bracelet: Open the first link of the copper chain with your chain-nose pliers, and slide on half of the toggle clasp and one charm. Close the link. Add a charm for each link of the chain. When you reach the last link, slide on one charm and the other half of the toggle clasp. Close the link.

Designer's Tip

If you can't find copper chain with links that open, use regular chain and string the copper wire through each chain link before making the second loop.

barter bead choker

All bangles jingle
when you move.
Here's one that
goes ka-ching!
It's made with
real African trade
beads, a form of
barter currency.

Instructions

Designer: Andrea L. Stern

Finished Size

24 inches (61 cm) long

Materials

15 head pins

30 blue pony beads, size 6/0

28 striped pony beads, size 3/0

40 Czech glass rondelles, 6 mm

8 Mexican ceramic tubes, 15 x 8 mm

14 sequins, 5 mm

14 red Czech round beads, 6 mm

7 African trade beads, ranging from 20 x 9 mm to 25 x 11 mm

Necklace wire, 24 inches (61 cm) long

Hook-and-eye clasp or a hook and split ring

72 white heart pony beads, size 6/0

26 ceramic barrel beads, 4 x 5 mm

Tools

Wire cutters

Round-nose pliers

Ruler or tape measure

Crimping pliers

1. Make a Mexican ceramic dangle by stringing beads onto a head pin in the following order:
   • Blue pony bead
   • Striped bead
   • Rondelle
   • Mexican ceramic tube
   • Rondelle
   • Striped bead
   • Blue pony bead
   Bend the top of the head pin 90° and use the wire cutters to trim to ¼ inch (6 mm). Using the round-nose pliers, make a simple loop. Repeat the pattern seven more times to make a total of eight dangles.

2. Make the African trade bead dangles by stringing onto a head pin as follows:
   • Blue pony bead
   • Sequin
   • 6-mm red round bead
   • African trade bead
   • 6-mm red round bead
   • Sequin
   • Blue pony bead
   Bend the top of head pin 90° and use the wire cutters to trim to ¼ inch (6 mm). Using the round-nose pliers, make a simple loop. Repeat the pattern six more times to make a total of seven dangles.

3. Use the wire cutters to cut a 24-inch (6.1 cm) length of necklace wire. With the round-nose pliers, make a simple loop at the end of the necklace wire, stringing the hook end of the clasp on before closing the loop with the crimping pliers.

4. String 10 of the white heart pony beads, and then push to the end of the wire.

5. String the following pattern six times:
   • Rondelle
   • Striped bead
   • Rondelle
   • White heart bead
   • Ceramic barrel bead
   • White heart bead

6. Slide a Mexican ceramic dangle onto the wire, followed by one white heart bead, one ceramic barrel bead, and one white heart bead.

7. Repeat step 6 a total of five times.

8. Next, string one rondelle, one striped bead, and one rondelle.

9. String 10 white heart beads.

10. Push all the beads to the end with the loop, making sure they are fairly snug. Use the round-nose pliers to bend the wire 90° (or as much as possible; it's really stiff wire). Trim the wire to ¼ inch (6 mm). Make a simple loop, and then add the eye piece of the clasp or the split ring. Close the loop with crimping pliers.

the good earth

A peaceful face beams from the pendant of this happy combination of turquoise, coral, bone, and antiqued brass.

Designer: Candie Cooper

Finished Size

Necklace: 15 inches (38.1 cm) long
Earrings: 1¼ inches (3.2 cm) long

Materials

Multipurpose adhesive

Antiqued brass filigree component

Turquoise tagua nut pendant

Faux bone face bead, 15 mm

Wet/dry sandpaper (optional)

Antiqued copper filigree flower

1 antiqued brass ½-inch (1.3 cm) square jump ring

1¼-yard length (approximately 1.1 m) red suede lace

Green seed beads

Beading wire, 19 strand

18 round coral beads, 4 mm

2 brass scrimp findings, 4 mm

2 antiqued brass pepper charms

4 brass spacer beads, 4 mm

2 faux bone bicone beads, 10 mm

2 antiqued brass square jump rings, ¼ inch (6 mm)

2 brass ribbon end findings with loop

2 antiqued brass jump rings, 6 mm

Brass hook finding

2 brass head pins

4 brass spacer beads, 5 mm

2 faux bone round beads, 10 mm

2 ear wires

Instructions

1. First, create the focal pendant. Use the multipurpose adhesive to glue the smaller antiqued brass filigree component on top of the tagua nut pendant so that the holes are aligned. Next, glue the faux bone face bead in the center of the filigree piece. (If your bead isn't flat-backed, sand until flat with wet/dry sandpaper and a little water.)

2. String the copper filigree flower onto the ½-inch (1.3 cm) square jump ring, followed by the nut/small filigree piece. Use the flat-nose pliers to close the ring so that it's snug. String the jump ring onto the red suede lace.

3. String 12 green seed beads onto the beading wire, followed by a coral bead and a scrimp finding. Thread the short side of the beading wire through the coral bead and scrimp to create a loop. Remove the slack in the seed bead loop, and tighten the scrimp finding. String one coral bead, one pepper charm, one coral bead, one 4-mm brass spacer bead, one bone bead, one 4-mm brass spacer bead, and five coral beads onto the beading wire, followed by the focal pendant. Finish by stringing the same beads and charms in reverse order on the other side of the focal pendant.

Tools

Flat-nose pliers

Scissors

Round-nose pliers

Wire cutters

4. Connect a ¼-inch (6 mm) square jump ring to each of the seed bead loops. Thread the suede lace through the jump ring on the left side, and bring the two ends together. Tie an overhand knot, and slide it up against the jump ring.

5. At this point the length of the necklace is adjustable. Use the scissors to cut the tails to your desired length, taking into account the clasp length. Finish the ends of the suede lace with the ribbon end findings. Attach the hook to the two ribbon end findings with two 6-mm jump rings.

6. To make the first earring, thread the following onto one of the head pins: one 5-mm spacer bead, one faux bone round bead, one 5-mm spacer bead, two green seed beads, one coral bead, and six seed beads. Use the round-nose pliers to make a small loop just above the last seed bead, and trim any excess with the wire cutters. Add one of the earring wires to the loop, and use the flat-nose pliers to firmly close the loop. Repeat this step to make the second earring.

Designer's Tip

You can age your brass findings by holding them in an open flame for a few seconds, and then quenching them in cold water.

eastern memories

The materials list here is just a suggestion. The items on your own brooch will depend on where you travel and what beads and baubles catch your eye.

Instructions

Designer: Candie Cooper

Finished Size

Approximately 2½ x 4 inches
(6.4 x 10.2 cm)

Materials

3 flat round wooden beads, 15 mm

Paper adhesive/glaze

Decorative paper

Antique copper slide frame and glass, 1½-inch (3.8 cm) square

Images for framed collage

Themed rubber stamps and ink pad (optional)

Safety-pin finding with 4 loops

Assorted copper findings: jump rings, eye pins, and head pins

Assorted small round spacers, Swarovski crystals, and seed beads

Assorted charms

Decorated felt ball bead

Flat-back crystals (optional)

Gold leaf (optional)

Tools

Small paintbrush

Scissors

Ruler

Toothpick

Chain-nose pliers

Round-nose pliers

Wire cutters

1. To decorate the flat round wooden beads, use the small paintbrush to paint a thin layer of paper adhesive onto one side of the bead. Set onto the back side of a small piece of the decorative paper and let dry. Use the scissors to trim the paper around the bead, leaving a 0.1- to 0.2-inch (3 to 4 mm) border. Cut slits around the edge to create tabs. Slide the bead onto a toothpick so that you can hold on to it. Paint the glue around the edge of the bead and roll the paper over. Repeat this process for the opposite side of the bead. Seal the entire bead with a coat of glue.

2. Anything can go into your slide frame, from a ticket stub to an image from a postcard or one that you've rubber-stamped. Place whatever images you've chosen or created back-to-back, and then sandwich them between the two pieces of glass. Trim away excess paper, and slide into the copper frame.

3. Use a jump ring to connect the frame to the middle loop on the safety-pin finding.

4. String the wooden and felt beads onto head pins and eye pins. Seed beads, Swarovski crystals, and the round copper beads can also be strung onto the eye pins. Finish by making simple loops, using the chain-nose and round-nose pliers. Use the wire cutters to trim the wire.

5. Connect the beaded links and charms to the remaining loops on the safety-pin finding. If your brooch is reversible, you can affix flat-back crystals or gold leaf to the backs of charms to make them two-sided.

bloodstone

A reddish form of chalcedony, carnelian is a stone that is found in royal Sumerian bead cloaks, ancient Roman signet rings, and this classic bracelet.

Instructions

Designer: Andrea L. Stern

Finished Size

8 inches (20.3 cm) long

Materials

1-foot (30.5 cm) length of 24-gauge sterling silver wire, or 5 silver head pins, each 3 inches long (7.6 cm)

8 matte coral seed beads, size 6/0

18 Chinese turquoise discs, 8 mm

8 brown ceramic discs, 8 mm

8 aqua white heart India glass barrel beads, 6 mm

Large carnelian or agate round bead, approximately 15 to 18 mm

Magnetic clasp

Tools

Ruler or tape measure

Round-nose pliers

Wire cutters

Designer's Tip

The magnetic clasp likes to grab onto any of the metal, which is why you want to put it on last in step 8.

1. Use the round-nose pliers to make a loop at one end of the silver wire by bending it at a 90° angle, approximately ¼ inch (6 mm) from the end.

2. String a seed bead, a Chinese turquoise disc, a ceramic disc, a Chinese turquoise disc, and a seed bead onto the wire. Bend the wire at a 90° angle, and use the wire cutters to cut it approximately ¼ inch (6 mm) from the bend. Using the round-nose pliers, make a simple loop, closing it as close to the end bead as possible.

3. Make a loop at one end of the rest of the long piece of wire, but before closing it, attach the first piece so that it dangles from the end of the loop.

4. String a barrel bead, a Chinese turquoise disc, a ceramic disc, a Chinese turquoise disc, and a barrel bead onto the long piece of wire. Make a simple loop as in step 2.

5. Repeat steps 2 through 4 one time, attaching each new link to the link before it. You now have four links on your bracelet.

6. String a Chinese turquoise disc, the big carnelian bead, and a Chinese turquoise disc, and make a loop.

7. Now, alternate barrel bead/turquoise disc/ceramic disc/turquoise disc/ barrel bead links with the seed bead/turquoise disc/ceramic disc/ turquoise disc/seed bead links, attaching them in reverse order so that they're a mirror image of the links on the other side of the big carnelian bead link. You should have a total of nine links on your bracelet.

8. Open the loop at one end and slide the magnetic clasp on. Close the loop. Repeat on the other end.

9. If you choose to use head pins instead, simply make the loops in the same manner. You can expect to get about two links per head pin.

flowers in winter

You close this choker by looping a hook into any of the links in a chain, making it easy to adjust the length to whatever you find most comfortable.

Instructions

Designer: Jamie Cloud Eakin

Finished Size

19¾ inches (50.2 cm) long

Materials

50 inches (127 cm) of flexible beading wire

16 crimp beads

5-to-1 loop finding

51 round white opaque beads, 4 mm

2 grams white opaque seed beads, size 11/0

9 Chinese porcelain round beads, 6 mm

10 Chinese porcelain round beads, 8 mm

6 jump rings, 5 mm

12 Chinese porcelain coins, 9 x 4 mm

2 Chinese porcelain barrels, 9 x 14 mm

2 Chinese porcelain round beads, 13 mm

2 Chinese porcelain teardrops, 12 x 22 mm

2 Chinese porcelain round beads, 15 mm

1 Chinese porcelain round bead, 20 mm

Hook

4-inch (10.2 cm) chain, 6 x 8 mm links

Head pin, 1½ inches (3.8 cm) long

Tools

Ruler

Wire cutters

Crimping pliers

2 needle-nose pliers

1. To begin making the fringed pendant, use the wire cutters to cut 4 inches (10.2 cm) of flexible wire. Pick up one crimp bead and loop the wire through the center loop of the finding's 5-loop section. Use the crimping pliers to crimp near the finding, trimming so the end will fit under a 4-mm white bead.

2. Add one 4-mm white bead, 25 seed beads, one 4-mm white bead, one 6-mm round bead, one 4-mm white bead, one 8-mm round bead, one 4-mm white bead, and one crimp bead. Move the beads up to adjust the tension, but make sure it's not too tight—you want the fringe to be flexible. Crimp the crimp bead, and trim near the crimp.

3. Cut 6 inches (15.2 cm) of flexible wire. Pick up a crimp bead and go through a loop next to the center loop on the finding. Pull the other end of the wire through the loop so there are 3 inches (7.6 cm) on each side. Crimp near the finding (figure 1).

fig. 1

4. On the strand closer to the center, add 25 seed beads, one 4-mm white bead, one 6-mm round bead, one 4-mm white bead, one 8-mm round bead, one 4-mm white bead, and one crimp bead. Move the beads up to adjust the tension (remember, not too tight). Crimp the crimp bead, and trim near the crimp.

5. On the other strand, repeat step 4, only this time use 21 seed beads.

6. Repeat steps 3 through 5 for the first loop on the other side of the finding's center loop.

7. For the last loops on each side, repeat steps 3 to 5 with the following changes: Use only 5 inches (12.7 cm) of wire, pulled through the loop so there are 2½ inches (6.4 cm) on each side. One of these strands uses 17 seed beads; the other, 14 seed beads. Finish the pendant by using the flat-nose pliers to open two jump rings for extra strength and stability and attach them to the top of the finding. (It's usually easier and faster than using a split ring.)

8. To begin stringing the necklace, cut 22 inches (55.9 cm) of wire.

9. Pick up one crimp and nine seed beads. String back through the crimp to create a loop. Adjust the tension, and crimp the crimp bead. Trim the end so it will fit under a 4-mm white bead.

10. String the necklace with beads in the following order:
- *4-mm white bead
- Coin

Repeat five times from *, then continue stringing beads as follows:
- 4-mm white bead
- Barrel
- 4-mm white bead
- 13-mm round bead
- 4-mm white bead
- Teardrop
- 4-mm white bead
- 15-mm round bead
- 4-mm white bead

11. Now pick up the 20-mm round bead and 21 seed beads. Thread the wire through the jump rings attached to the fringed finding. (If your jump ring doesn't slide over your seed beads, add 10 seeds, the jump rings, and then another 10 seeds to center the fringed pendant.) Go through the 20-mm round again to create a loop, as illustrated in figure 2.

fig. 2

12. Pick up beads as in step 10, except in reverse order.

13. Repeat step 9.

14. Use two jump rings to attach the hook to one side of the necklace and two jump rings to attach the chain to the other side.

15. Add an 8-mm round bead and a 4-mm white bead on the head pin. Use the needle-nose pliers to wrap the wire around the end section of the chain to finish.

Jeannette Chiang Bardi has had a passion for making jewelry ever since she discovered the amazing world of crystals and gemstones. She's inspired by the incredible history of jewelry and has integrated ancient symbolism and techniques into her work. Jeannette is especially fascinated by ancient Egyptian and Chinese jewelry, from the history of wire wrapping to the mystical use of crystals and stones.

Francie Broadie has been beading and fusing glass for the last 10 years. She has a master's degree in art, and she teaches beading at several bead stores. When she's not teaching, she beads full time. You can find her work at www.franciebroadie.com, through which you can also contact her. In between beading projects, Francie often has to chase her cat around the house yelling, "Beads are not for kitties!"

Jean Campbell is a craft author and editor whose specialty is beading and jewelry design. She was the founding editor of *Beadwork* magazine and has written and edited more than 12 beading books, including *The Art of Beaded Beads* and *Beading with Crystals*, both from Lark Books. Her artwork has been in several shows, including the Miyuki Delica Challenge's Myths and Folktales and the Suburban Fine Arts Center's Object Beadwork. She lives in Minneapolis, Minnesota.

Candie Cooper specializes in creating accessible mixed media jewelry and crafts. She is the author of *Felted Jewelry* (Lark Books, 2007), which features 20 fabulous felted projects including necklaces, rings, and bracelets. Candie currently lives and works in Shenzhen, China. Visit her website at www.candiecooper.com for a further look at her creations and for a link to her online journal, The Savvy Crafter.

Sherry Duquet believes that jewelry should be whimsical and expressive. "I am inspired by the brilliance of natural gemstones," she says. "When you put on a piece of jewelry, it should make you want to sing out loud." Since starting Solstice Designs with a fellow designer, Sherry has developed a loyal following. To see more of her work, visit her virtual storefront at www.solsticed.etsy.com.

Jamie Cloud Eakin is a professional bead artist, teacher, and perpetual student of her craft. She is the author of *Beading with Cabochons* and the upcoming *Bugle Bead Bonanza* (both from Lark Books). Jamie has won numerous awards for her beadwork. To view the pieces she creates in her Modesto, California, studio, go to www.studiojamie.com.

Elizabeth Glass Geltman and **Rachel Geltman** are the mother-daughter design team behind Geltman Jewelry Designs, LLC. Their work has been published in books like *500 Earrings* and *New Directions in Metal Clay* (both from Lark Books), as well as in other publications, such as *Bead Bugle*, *Bead Release*, *Jewelry Arts & Lapidary Journal*, *PMC Connection*, *Studio PMC*, and the *Washington Post*.

Catherine Hodge is fond of Japanese cluster earrings, frame purses, and peep-toe shoes. She blends her love of femininity with texture and nautical influences in her jewelry. Catherine has had jewelry designs featured in national beading magazines, even though she's still studying at Kendall College of Art and Design. Check out her jewelry at www.catherinemarissa.com or catherinemarissa.etsy.com.

Cindy Kinerson is a self-taught bead artist and basket weaver. Now she and her husband own a bead and jewelry supply store, where Cindy designs jewelry and teaches beading workshops. She finds inspiration in long walks, beautiful gardens, antique shops, museums, and especially in the artwork of her daughters and nieces. Her designs have appeared in national publications and in several galleries.

Elizabeth Larsen works as a biologist for Snohomish County, Washington. She started beading as a hobby to challenge her creative side. Little did she know how her passion would blossom. Elizabeth began making jewelry in 2001 after taking a class in chainware from a local bead store. She uses this technique to create bold yet feminine pieces of art and jewelry.

Karen J. Lauseng is an internationally recognized New Mexico artist whose artwork has appeared in many books, including *The Art of Jewelry: Wood* and *500 Earrings* (both from Lark Books). *Art Jewelry Magazine* featured her work on its front cover. She has displayed her pieces in more than 100 venues, including solo exhibitions, juried shows, and galleries. See for yourself at www.kjartworks.com.

Marilyn Peters is on the Board of Directors of the Bead Society of Northern California, and she helps put on two major bead shows annually in Oakland. She also teaches at the B.A.B.E. Bead Show every year, as well as at her local bead store every Saturday, to share her knowledge of stitches, color, composition, and techniques. She has had two pieces featured in the online *Bead-Patterns Magazine*.

Andrea L. Stern grew up surrounded by artists, so she knew she'd make some kind of art. She started with drawings, and then moved on to painting, beadwork, and quilting. When she opened her own bead business, she learned to apply the principles of design she had learned in school. You can find samples of her work on her blog (andibeads.blogspot.com) and website (www.embellishmentcafe.com).

Terry Taylor is an acquisitions editor at Lark Books. He's also the author of several books, including *Altered Art*, *Artful Paper Dolls*, *The Altered Object*, and *Button! Button!* (all published by Lark Books). He's a jeweler in his spare time and prefers to spend his vacations taking metalworking classes. His other passion requires him to fly around the country to see well-known opera companies perform.

Mike Ann Zable is an Alaskan designer known as the Stone Age Diva. A retired florist, she delights in collecting ethnic art and beads. Through a relationship with Fair Trade ventures, she helps impoverished African women earn a living wage. Mike Ann's pieces include some ageless elements of the continent. She likes knowing that her unique designs use beads made by Third World women and artists.

acknowledgments

Deborah Coule is the owner of Chevron Trading Post & Bead Co. (www.chevronbeads.com), a wonderful bead store in Asheville, North Carolina. Deborah was gracious and generous in sharing her knowledge about world beads with our book team and lending us many precious beads for photography.

Beth Sweet aided me greatly in the book's development, helping to curate jewelry designs and shape the book's content. Art director Megan Kirby reinvigorated the *Beading with* series design with colorful new forms and dramatic photography by Stewart O'Shields, and J'aime Allene Perkins created the book's fine illustrations. Megan was assisted in layout and design by the talented team of Carol Morse, Jeff Hamilton, and Meagan Shirlen. In production editorial, Larry Shea and Mark Bloom did excellent and essential work bringing all the elements together smoothly, adding valuable content, and creating a seamless package.

Above all, I'd like to thank the 16 beaders whose elegant jewelry is featured in these pages. Their delightful creative efforts provided the motivation for producing the book. I hope these projects inspire you to create your own jewelry designs; if they do, please visit www.larkbooks.com to share photos of your world-bead jewelry on our website.

—Ray Hemachandra, senior editor